Human Resources
or was it
Human Remains?

ANDREW WYNDHAM

ISBN:-10: 1502819406
ISBN-13: 978-1502819406

DEDICATION

To my truly wonderful parents for their love, belief and
empowerment.

CONTENTS

1 SETTING THE SCENE

A Human Resources department is often seen as a necessary evil in an organisation. On one hand it is the filtration system through which people pass on route to starting their exciting new career. On the other hand it can act as the muscle through which employees are expelled at the premature end of their career. In the intervening period of employment the role of the HR department can vary from that of a nurturing parent to that of a corrective head teacher.

Few people regard a visit to their HR office as anything better than a visit to their dentist or indeed, to a Police Station. Too frequent contact with HR normally means that something is going seriously wrong at work.

The image of an HR Manager is normally that of someone who is fairly `stuffy`, and who works in an atmosphere where they have to be `whiter than white`. It wouldn`t do for someone in HR to be seen to falling below the required standard, particularly when they may be required to discipline colleagues for exactly the same thing.

Some would also anticipate that a day packed with one interview after another can be very boring. Indeed, let`s face it, it is! Nevertheless, over time the very nature and variety of HR work presents many weird and wonderful situations, and this book documents some of the true stories that have happened to me in my twenty year career working for some of the largest employers in the UK.

When I started the role that is now known as `Human Resources` was more commonly known as `Personnel`. Indeed I was initially employed as a Personnel Officer before the profession re-branding to `Human Resources` took place. Indeed some of my experience is now extremely old indeed and pre-dates some of the more politically correct changes in the workplace. In the meantime whilst much employment legislation has changed, many aspects of human behaviour have not, and will not.

Just when I feel that I have seen every possible employment permutation, someone, somewhere, will do something totally unique. Long may that continue. Names have been changed to protect the innocent, otherwise the stories are true.

2 EMPLOYING ALL SORTS OF FOLK

The first impression that an employer will gain from a prospective employee is from their letter of approach and the accompanying curriculum vitae. The quality of that initial contact is so important in convincing an employer that an application should be pursued, particularly when it is compared with the numerous other professionally produced applications which tend to flood in.

When advertising for staff the key challenge is to obtain a response from a small number of well matched candidates, rather than say, a huge number of people who only possessed partial skills for the job. If spelling is not your best attribute, it makes sense to get a friend to check your approach letter. This tactic was obviously not employed by a lady with an oriental name who wrote to me to apply for a position of an admin assistant.

It will come as no surprise to learn that when responding to an advertisement for an admin job the letter of application is even more important than usual. As this position involved working for the Regional Audit Manager, the Regional Security Manager and myself, I had carefully worded the advertisement to make it clear that we were looking for an experienced administrator who was able to type at 40 words per minute but was capable of a high degree of accuracy and more importantly, paying attention to detail.

At the time Wang word processors were state of the art and in this particular letter of application I was somewhat surprised that this lady stated that she was very good at `tying` and had a great deal of experience with a `wank` word processor !!!

Now either the word processor was of poor quality and she had decided to be brutally honest or her spelling and attention to detail had not quite reached the required standard! Needless to say those were the days before spell checkers were common currency.

***

It is however the case that the inability to spell was not restricted to job applicants. I spent some time working for a large security organisation and by and large they always promoted from within. Now this organisation employed many excellent employees including numerous fine ex-service personnel. There were however occasions when recruitment in this industry proved difficult and it was almost necessary to employ some people who had turned to security work as a last resort. After all, in those days the hours were 60 per week in 12 hour shifts, and the pay was poor. If people could find employment elsewhere they frequently did.

One senior employee was a charismatic Regional Operations Manager. He was one of those larger than life characters who was extremely good when dealing with people in spite of the fact that he had risen up the ranks from humble beginnings. He was responsible for around 250 separate business units and for turnover that ran into millions of pounds. This was an important role which geographically stretched from Birmingham to Cornwall and along the South Coast to Southampton. Throughout the region there were approximately two thousand employees were employed in his region.

This individual was highly skilled at getting the best out of his staff, the sort of individual who would lead his people in any charge over the trenches and they would blindly follow at his behest. His Achilles heel was that he struggled to spell his own job title.

On many occasions he would be required to authorise paperwork for matters such as overtime. At these times he was normally asked to sign and print his name and to spell his job title. Unfortunately he was totally incapable of spelling the job title to which he had been promoted and the best he could manage was the unfortunate habit of spelling it Regional `Apparitions` Manager. Goodness only knows what the accounts department thought we were employing out in the field.

He seemed to get away with his spelling issues on internal company business but it became an issue if he was working late and had to send out an urgent letter without the help of his secretary. One letter went out to a key business contact from the `Regonal Apparations Manger`. Indeed I`d heard it said that one customer thought that he had done well as they used to work with him when he was a `Dumper Driver`.

***

I always take a very keen interest in what is written on an application form and particularly on the section where applicants detail their hobbies and interests outside of work. Quite often I find that this can give an indication of whether they would fit in with others working in that department.

Now some applicants tend to use the scattergun approach and list every hobby known to man in the hope that the reader will tune into at least one of them. Indeed I recall a line manager being persuaded to employ the most unsuitable applicant for a job on the basis that the prospective employee shared his passion for marathon running. To the manager the characteristics of determination and endurance seemed perfect for someone in a sales career. Unfortunately however it proved that the individual was more determined to spend all his time training for his event! It is therefore the case that the scattergun approach can sometimes backfire as the reader wonders how they would actually find time to fit work into their busy life.

Now being a simple fellow I enjoy golf and music and am not afraid to happily list those interests on an application. Others however are inclined to do different things with their time and I must confess that over the years I still found it fairly shocking that on two occasions candidates have found it necessary to list `sex` as a hobby! Whilst I can appreciate their interest in the subject, some things are best left unsaid, or indeed, unwritten.

5

One of the above individuals was applying for a job in the security industry. This is a notoriously difficult industry for which to recruit and it was with a large degree of irony that he was the only candidate for the vacancy, and proceeded to get the job. The 60 hour week may however have had the effect of cutting down his recreation, and indeed, procreation, time!

It may or may not surprise you that interestingly the other applicant to list `sex` as a hobby was a female!

***

Unfortunately there are those people who struggle with literacy and if given an application form would ask a relative to complete it for them. This is not normally a big issue for certain positions such as working as a machinist or on most production lines. I have however known it where an individual used his immaculate application form to successfully secure a position as a parcel delivery driver. A week into the job his supervisor had received numerous complaints about undelivered parcels and it didn`t take long for him to realise that he had employed an illiterate driver who was not capable of reading the address label. In future all applicants were required to complete their application form in the presence of the supervisor!

***

Another of those interesting parts of the application form which can throw up some strange responses involves the section where an individual is asked to declare any `non-spent` convictions. The UK Rehabilitation of Offenders Act 1974 aims to help offenders to reintegrate into society by ensuring that, in certain circumstances, their criminal conviction should, in effect, be expunged.

The basic principle of the Act was that, following a certain period of time, all convictions (except those resulting in prison sentences of over 30 months) are regarded as `spent` and the offender is a `rehabilitated person`. This period of time depends on the sentence imposed. A rehabilitated person is treated largely as though they had not committed, been charged with, prosecuted for, convicted of or sentenced for the offence. In most circumstances the convicted person does not have to reveal the conviction or admit its existence.

In my time I have seen a number of job applicants declaring serious convictions including GBH and manslaughter although I feel that such `honest` declarations are probably disproportionately on the low side. My instinct tells me that in reality most people keep such bad news to themselves in the belief that an employer faced with ten equally qualified candidates is unlikely to go for the person who declares that they have been convicted of manslaughter.

One candidate I interviewed at a recruitment open day described in some detail how he had acquired his GBH conviction. Apparently someone had looked at him in the wrong way and he had lost his temper and `given them a kicking`. I thought for a moment about the number of customers who would not only look at him the wrong way but also talk to him in the wrong way. On this occasion I chose not to take the chance to employ him and suspected that this individual did not actually want the job and was merely going through the motions to appease those who were monitoring his attempts to find work under the Job Seekers rules.

***

Unless you are a friend of the Managing Director or have always been self-employed, an interview is something that we have all been through. It never ceases to amaze me what people actually say in an interview situation. I recall one such scenario when I was working for a large retail company. I needed to recruit a PA who would be working for two of the functional Regional Management team [Security and Audit] and myself. We occupied some offices above one of the retail stores and worked very closely as a unit. The PA was required to effectively organise our diaries and undertake some secretarial and administrative work.

At that particular time the economy was buoyant and in fairly full employment and from our advertisement we didn`t exactly get a high number of suitable candidates. As a result we interviewed one or two candidates who probably wouldn`t normally have made it. One such individual had an appointment towards the end of the interview day.

The interview was going fairly well until we got to her reason for leaving her previous employment. With a surprising degree of honestly she declared that her husband had GBH`d her former manager because he did not like her working with men.

Now there was no reason for the job advertisement to specifically mention that she would be working with male colleagues and when I informed her that she would be working with three males in our office, unlike myself, she showed no flicker of concern.

I hurriedly moved on to ask her about her hobbies and interests and was surprised to see that in her spare time she was a keen medium. For a split second I pondered whether this line of communication could come in very useful in the future for communicating with any future male managers! As the interview draw to a close, it was with a degree of trepidation that I escorted her to the front door where she was to be collected by her waiting husband.

***

I recall another occasion one early November when a Mr Singh was booked in for an interview at 2pm on the Wednesday after the clocks had gone back an hour. He did not arrive and I put it down to the fact that he had not had the courtesy to advise me that he wished to cancel. I carried on with some other work and then exactly one hour later at 3pm I received a call from my secretary. She advised that Mr Singh had arrived for his interview. It was only after speaking to him for a few minutes that I realised that he had not changed his watch for the previous few days and had been carrying on to his own time!!!

***

When conducting an interview I always tended to follow the current HR `best practice`. At the time it was taboo to interview across a table as this provided a psychological barrier between the interviewer and interviewee. This meant that I was in the habit of setting the room up with two chairs in the centre of the room. Naturally this left a space around the two chairs.

On one occasion I had an appointment to interview a Mr Smith for a job as a machinist in the factory. This particular role involved being seated for most of the working day and in common with every job on the production line, it was essential that the job was completed otherwise the line would slow or completely stop.

Mr Smith was shown to my office and I welcomed him in and invited him to sit down. In order to settle the nerves of candidates, I usually spent a couple of minutes on `chit chat`, for example asking them if their journey went well, or perhaps if they had any difficulties in finding the office etc. I would then tell them a little about the company before moving on to ask them about their most recent employment.

This particular interview was routine and had been going very well for about fifteen minutes until suddenly Mr Smith rose out of his seat and started to walk around the room. I immediately thought that he was about leave however this wasn`t the case at all. Instead he continued to answer the question but did so whilst pacing around the outside of the room. Believe me it is disconcerting to conduct an interview when at times the interviewee is actually behind you. He completed two laps before I gently asked him to sit down as I was becoming dizzy.

***

Whilst on the subject of gaining employment, I hope that you don`t mind at this point me mentioning a story conveyed to me by Ron, a former neighbour. Unfortunately for Ron he had been made redundant from his sales role at time when the economy was going through a tough time. Where we lived unemployment was approaching 10% and there were very few opportunities.

Not being one to live within his means, his credit cards were under serious pressure and he was fairly desperate to secure another position as a sales representative as soon as he possibly could. The general state of the economy meant that there was huge competition for any work which became available. I recall advertising a retail sales position locally at that time and getting 400 applicants. Many of these were from overqualified candidates but who were desperate to find work.

Now Ron had contacted every employment agency he could think of and had managed to obtain a total of twelve interviews. By any standard this was a very bright start to his campaign. Given the success of his initial prospecting he was confident that both he and his skills were in high demand at that he would be able to `pick and choose` from the available positions.   He also felt able to drive a hard bargain with regard to his salary demands.

The interviews came and went and Ron waited by the phone for the offers to flood in.   After six unsuccessful interviews he decided to radically alter his aggressive negotiating stance on salary.   He was now more conciliatory and had moved from demanding a high salary and bonus to merely asking for a moderate salary plus a review in three months time.   During the first three months he would show them that he was indispensable and would prove that it made good sense to pay him well to keep him in the business.

After a number of weeks, the expected offers had not rolled in and he was starting to become more concerned.   Nevertheless, there were a couple of very desirable positions available from the remaining six interviews.   In the meantime he missed a couple of mortgage payments at a time when property prices were falling, his house had moved into negative equity and his credit cards had all reached their limit.

It wasn`t long before a couple of interviews had been cancelled and there were only two positions left.   As is the case with multiple job applications, timing is all important.   Whilst you need a job, there is always the possibility that you may be offered a `bum` job before the job that you really wants arrives.

This can represent a major dilemma and indeed another friend of mine in similar circumstances accepted a position and arrived for work on the Monday.   When he telephoned his wife at lunchtime she confirmed that he had received a written offer letter from the preferred organisation that morning.   One morning`s loyalty did not count for much and he immediately resigned in order to accept for the new offer!

Anyway back to Ron.   He did receive an offer for a `bum job`.   On offer was a small salary, potentially high commission but little job satisfaction.   Although desperate, Ron was a bit of a gambler and he elected to turn down the offer of the bum job [well at least he didn`t accept and then let them down!].   That left him with the final job from the list of twelve vacancies. He attended a local interview with an employment agency and was quickly granted a second interview at the head office which was approximately 3 hours drive away. By now the pressure was becoming intense and the desperation was beginning to show. He had one opportunity and no second chances. He was even buying his groceries on his maxed out credit cards.

In preparation for the interview, Ron spent hours researching the organisation. He understood their products, their marketplace, their customers and their key competitors. He used one of my favourite rules for attending an interview, `always know more about the organisation than the interviewer is likely to know`. He had attended the local library and accessed business directories giving him figures for turnover and profit and loss, these were now ingrained on his memory. Not only that but all of the names of the directors were at his fingertips, as were the key office locations. Furthermore he had prepared and rehearsed a fantastic presentation and even arranged for his best suit to be dry cleaned for the occasion.

On the day of the interview Ron arose at the crack of dawn to give enough time for two rehearsals of his presentation.   He left his house allowing an extra hour for the long journey to be absolutely certain that he had built in some flexibility in case of traffic delays. After driving for about and hour and a half, he decided to stop and get himself a coffee.   He reached into the back of his car to where he normally kept his jacket, hanging neatly on a peg. No jacket.

Cue a moment of anger mixed with a degree of panic. There was no chance whatsoever of turning around and going home, he was already half way there.   He quickly decided that his best policy would be to come clean with the interviewer, and make a bit of a joke about the situation.   Perhaps he could use this tactic to establish rapport with his interviewer.

Somewhat reassured, he headed into the service area and ordered himself a coffee. As he was nervous and felt the need to comfort eat, he also treated himself to a fresh doughnut. His mind was far away when he sat down and took a vigorous bite and splat! The doughnut all but exploded and the sweet strawberry jam burst out and went all over his nicely pressed shirt. Disaster!

For a busy Sales Director, seeing a prospective jacketless Sales Representative, covered in strawberry jam, must have provided light relief during a day of otherwise wall to wall routine interviewees. Ron's interview lasted all of 15 minutes, following which his travelling expenses were briefly agreed and then he was shown the door. It hadn't been a good day at the office.

***

Over the years I had managed to cultivate a poker face so that if at any time someone said or did something which surprised me, they probably would not have twigged from my lack of reaction. One such occasion when I needed to use this skill was when I worked for the clothing manufacturing organisation. We were always desperate to recruit machinists and following an advertising campaign, I had managed to arrange some interviews with some college leavers.

One of the applicants was an extremely attractive young lady who presented in a very smart tight fitting skirt and blouse. The interview was going quite well and she drew my attention to the subject of her health and fitness. She told me that some months before she had been in a car accident. The interview took place many years before the Disability Discrimination Act came into force and I was a little concerned because in the factory we did not have a great record for sickness absence.

I enquired whether she still suffered any ill effects from the accident and she said 'Not now although I used to get pains here'. With that she prodded her sternum and in the course of doing so, obviously pressed on the poppers fastening her blouse. In a flash several poppers came open and the interviewing manager was exposed to….well…a significant amount of flesh. The poor girl could not have blushed more and hurriedly re-buttoned her blouse. This was indeed a time for me to adopt my poker face although I have to add that her application was successful!

Indeed this was not the only time that this sort of incident happened. On another occasion I was interviewing for the position of assistant manager in a retail office. The position had been advertised within the company and I was a little disappointed that there was only one applicant. My initial disappointment was however, eased by the fact that the cv provided by the applicant looked particularly good. It has always been the objective of any recruitment campaign to achieve a small number of very well qualified candidates. In that way you do not waste everyone's time and effort by interviewing numerous unqualified candidates who have no hope of being appointed to the position.

At that time I was responsible for HR matters in about 170 retail branches and whilst I constantly travelled around my region, the applicant who I'll call `Rosie Jones`, was one person I had yet to meet. Notwithstanding the fact that I had not met Rosie, in that sort of environment you do from time to time different rumours about various individuals and I had heard a whisper that she was someone who had a bit of a `glint in her eye`! That said, I always lived by the rule that I would take people as I found them and even if that was true, it would not necessarily affect her ability to do her job.

Rosie had a trip of around 100 miles to get to my office. She arrived exactly on time for her appointment and was greeted by my secretary Jill, who subsequently telephoned to confirm her arrival. I asked Jill to show Rosie up to my office. Shortly thereafter there was a knock at my door and both Jill and Rosie were standing there. Jill introduced me to Rosie and I immediately noticed that she was smartly dressed, albeit wearing a very short skirt for an interview.

I could see that Jill was holding a letter for me to sign so I asked Rosie to take a seat and I quickly signed the letter. As I turned to walk to my desk Rosie had her back to me and had made an attempt to sit down in her short skirt. For some reason her attempt at sitting had failed and she bounced back up to a standing position with her skirt having ridden up to waist level to completely reveal her bottom and a very small pair of panties!

Now I'm not entirely sure who had the redder face and still do not know to this day whether it was a pure accident or otherwise. All I do know is that after this initial incident the interview went very well and as the only candidate, Rosie was duly appointed to her new position!

***

Normally when applicants arrived for a job interview I would always try to greet them and on the walk to the room, engage them in conversation about a hobby or interest. To do so I usually checked their application form beforehand and scanned the section on hobbies and interests. It was always useful if we had something in common such a particular sport or perhaps music.

On one day I was interviewing for an assistant manager position in a large retail store. We had decided to interview both internal and external candidates and one of those people who had been invited worked for a rival company in a similar position. The interview room was in an office on the first floor and it involved quite a long walk to both collect the fellow and then return to the interview room.

Having first read his application, I could see that he was a musician and played in a band. On the walk to the room we were discussing music and he said that he had just obtained a PA system so that they could play before a live audience. At that point in time I too was interested in the subject and we briefly discussed the cost of a decent PA system.

As the interview drew to an end we again returned to the subject of PA systems and I asked whether the band had paid for their system by charging for gigs. At that point he became very excited and animated. He told me that he played in a church band, and he said, `What we did was to pray to the Lord and we were then provided with a PA system`.

I replied, `How does that work exactly?`

He replied `Well, we didn`t have the money for a PA so we decided to pray for a month. At the end of the month God arranged for us to receive enough money to pay for the PA`.

`I don`t understand ` I said.

He replied, `Well it was simple, we prayed and all of a sudden the church received a tax rebate and we were able to buy the PA`

Not being a religious person I was somewhat amazed by this statement and was forced to consider whether his Regional Manager would simply accept that he was praying for good sales figures!.

3 THAT TOUCHY ISSUE OF PERSONAL HYGIENE

In the 1980`s much of the UK clothing manufacturing business had been in serious decline and had been staggering around on its last legs for some time. Whilst it`s outward appearance was tidy, my factory was in a rough part of town and employed some people who did not feel that they could get employment anywhere else. This was probably more down to lack of feeling of self worth and opportunity rather than their inherent skills or ability.

Some of the skills within that factory were sublime. Anyone who has seen a skilled sewing machinist work will appreciate the speed and precision with which they work. Usually pitted against a strict work study based time limit for a particular job, they worked at breakneck speed with the sort of manual dexterity normally reserved for a top musician. I often wondered what some of them could have achieved, given a different start in life.

Whilst it was difficult to attract staff for machinist roles, certain jobs in the factory were more popular and attracted better pay and kudos. One of these positions was that of a cloth cutter and in my first week one of the cloth cutters retired at the age of sixty-five after 51 years service.

The workforce itself was 85% female with perhaps 30% of the overall total coming from ethnic minorities. In all of my career in HR, I cannot say that I met a group that I preferred to deal with than those people in that factory. They were honest, often brutally so.

Given that the working environment involved 200 people working quite physically in a confined space, the vexed subject of personal hygiene was frequently an issue. Indeed this subject raised its ugly head within about a week of me starting working at the factory in what was my first HR job.

I would however like to make clear a very important point right from the beginning of this chapter. Poor personal hygiene is not confined to any particular race, creed, social class or section of the community. In my experience I have dealt with poor examples of personal hygiene from *all* aforementioned areas. Indeed, during my working life I have had complaints about and from, individuals from all of the various racial groups. *It is therefore a problem affecting certain individuals.*

Now my predecessor as HR Manager had been sacked because she had upset the workforce. Now this in my experience was highly unusual. Normally it is the HR person who does the sacking, not the other way around!

Apparently this person had a reputation for behaving like the bossy and pompous headmistress of a school. This sort of approach did not go down well with a group of people who almost to a person were very fearful of schools and anyone who resembled the authority linked with such establishments.

The story I heard went that one morning had seen a lot of rain fall and as a result all of the staff had brought umbrellas into work. They were not allowed to take them on to the shop floor and therefore they had left them to dry in a corridor area outside. In the view of most fair minded people this was an eminently sensible thing to do given that they were wet, late for work and did not wish their lateness to cause their pay to be docked.

Unfortunately this commonsense view did not tally with that of the self appointed `headmistress`. As a result she had confiscated the umbrellas and locked them away in a side room. She had then disappeared off somewhere and the result was that when it came to lunch they were unable to retrieve their umbrellas and as a consequence some were drenched whilst taking their break. Oh dear.

Production was stopped and the Managing Director had little alternative but to dispense with the services of his HR Manager.

As I was aware of this background I was determined to get off on the right foot with the workforce and to treat them with fairness, respect and courtesy. I also did not think that it would be long before they tested me out. It came in the shape of Margaret, a senior machinist who had been brought up in the school of hard knocks. She was now a single parent who for many years had been in an abusive relationship. Nevertheless she had always worked and provided for her family and was someone upon whom the management could totally rely to get the job done and to do it well.

It was rare for Margaret to offer a smile and frankly, given her lot in life, who could blame her. Whilst hardened by life's experiences, no-one could accuse Margaret of being anything but extremely clean. Given that she worked in close proximity to 8-10 people, woe betide any of them if their personal hygiene fell below her acceptable standard.

Any prospective machinists that we managed to attract were given a manual dexterity test. This test was regarded as being more important than the interview as we were not particularly interested in someone who could talk particularly well. It was however important that they understood what the job involved and the environment that they would be working in.

Now Sukhbir was a seventeen year old Asian lad whom I had employed in my first week of working at the factory. I recall the interview particularly well as during that week I had a heavy cold and was dosed up with medication. He was a bright, pleasant young man who was very well turned out. It was his first job since leaving college and he was keen to impress and do well. In fact if anything I was concerned that he may get bored quite quickly and leave.

Sukhbir was allocated to work in Margaret's team so that she could show him the ropes. This was one of three teams which were under the responsibilities of one of the factory supervisors. His first day seemed to go well and without incident and at least no adverse comments reached me in my office which was located next to a production line on the floor below where Sukbir was working.

A short time into his second day there was a knock on my door and through the window I could see that it was Margaret. I opened the door and asked her to take a seat. With a face as hard as stone she said, `Either you tell him or we will`.

`Tell who`? I gently enquired.

`That Asian lad that *you* took on, he stinks, either you tell him or we will`.

Now I had heard that the peer group could be quite hard on people in these situations and typically an individual would return to their machine to find a number of `gifts` of deodorant or worse still, to be presented with some deodorant in front of everyone in the canteen.

Now either of these actions would have been potentially horrendous for a young man in his first job. Imagine if as a shy, seventeen year old, you were presented with deodorant in a canteen full of perhaps 150 people. It just did not bear thinking about.

`Margaret I`ll tell him, leave it to me` I said.

`When will you tell him, we cannot stand it any longer,` she replied.

`I`ll tell him by the end of the day, is that OK?` I added.

`As long as you do,` said Margaret. With that she left.

Now whilst I had heard of these issues within the work place I had never *actually* told anyone that they had smelled. This was going to be a first for me. I called Sukhbir`s supervisor and asked her to tell him that I would like to see him at lunchtime. I got myself a coffee and a notepad and settled down to plan my strategy for diplomatically breaking this news to the unfortunate young man.

At one minute past mid-day there was a knock on my office door and it was Sukhbir.

`Hi Sukhbir, come in and sit down, I just wanted to have a chat to see how things were going in your first couple of days. How are you getting on with the job?`

`Very well thank you,` he said.

`Is your supervisor showing you the ropes?` I asked.

`Oh yes she`s very helpful,` he replied.

`And are you getting to know your colleagues?` I enquired.

` Yes, I think so, I`m enjoying the work,` Sukhbir replied.

`That is excellent,` I said, `now there was one thing which I had forgotten to mention to you at interview and quite honestly that was my mistake.`

`What was that?` he said politely.

`It`s just about personal hygiene,` I said.

He nodded and added a confirming grunt.

`Well obviously the job can be quite physical and in the summer it gets very hot and we all sweat quite a bit. As you know you are all working quite close to each other and it is important that we pay close attention to your personal hygiene. Do you understand what I mean by this?`

Sukhbir replied `Yes, of course`.

`OK then,` I said, `so you will look after your personal hygiene, won`t you?`

`Yes, I will. No problem,` he enthusiastically replied.

`Thanks for your understanding,` I said, with a degree of relief. `I`m glad that things are going well so far,` and showed him out of the office.

I was really quite pleased with the way that our meeting had gone. I had studied his features for any sign that he was upset by what I had to say, but did not detect any. Indeed he seemed to take the advice with a great deal of maturity. This did not really surprise me as he seemed mature beyond his years and an intelligent young man.

Two days later it was with a degree of surprise when my secretary Jill, informed me that he had suddenly left the company. Whilst there was a great deal of labour turnover in clothing manufacturing, Sukhbir did not strike me as someone who would have not given the job at least a bit of time.

Jill`s office was immediately outside my door and she would normally act as the buffer between myself and the shop floor. She certainly saw everyone who came in and out, she said, `I remember him very well because he was the one who came down to see you 2 days ago wasn`t he?`

`Yes.` I replied.

`It was really strange what he said to me on his way out.` Jill said.

`What was that?` I replied.

`Well he asked me what "personal hygiene" meant,` she said.

Enough said, quite obviously my strategy for explaining this most touchy of subjects had not worked!

***

Following this setback for my techniques in the breaking of bad news regarding bad body odour, I decided review my communication strategy. I knew that this problem would not go away and it was only a matter of time before it occurred again.

Many of the shop floor supervisors had lived locally and grown up with the shop floor employees. Some of the older employees were immigrants and at times there was communication problem where English was not their first language. There was however an informal arrangement in place to deal with the lack of communication.

Very often the employees` children were born in the UK and it never ceased to amaze me where often the supervisor knew both the employee and their children, sometimes because they had attended the same local school as the employees` children. On occasions when a work related matter need explaining to someone, frequently this informal `network` was used to do it. The factory was generally a very happy place to work. The wide racial mix did not give rise to any significant problems and the fact that for many of the workforce English was not their first language, generally was not a problem.

Before my time the way that the issue of personal hygiene was often dealt with was that the shop floor supervisor would know the English born children of the employee and would give them a call to say words to the effect of `there's a bit of a problem with your mother could you have a gentle word please?` No offence was taken, the offspring would speak to them and the problem was resolved, if not always permanently, long enough to give a "breathing space".

Indeed one of those people with whom we had a constant hygiene problem was someone that I would assist from time to time with issues such as the understanding of documentation, payment of bills etc. She was very grateful for the help and she would often produce a small gift for me from her pocket at the start of the working day such as an apple or a wrapped boil sweet. Now I don't wish to sound unkind however I didn't always eat the apple!

I recall assisting her with various monetary issues from understanding her payslip to the paying of utility bills. These interactions would often make me smile because in her native country of Pakistan, whoever had taught her to speak the very few words of English that she possessed, had taught her to add the phrase `give it to me` if the sentence referred to an amount of money.

When explaining a problem with her electric bill she would put it something this;

`Electricity company want £100, give it to me, I paid £80, give it to me, in cash, give it to me, they say get a meter and pay £5 per week, give it to me...`.

Or a payslip query could be:

`Last week I earned £100 basic, give it to me, but lost national insurance of £10, give it to me, and tax of £15 give it to me, and £3 pension give it to me.....`.

She was quite a character and we enjoyed a lot of laughter when dealing with these issues!

**

Now back to my strategy for breaking bad news of this kind. It was fairly apparent that issues of employees giving off odours were generally for two reasons. It was either caused by:

 a] Certain foods and drinks, such as onions, garlic, curry, certain spicy foods, coffee, alcohol, or

b] Failure to wash themselves or their clothes.

Now when it came to telling the unfortunate victim, it seemed much more civilised to tell them that it was probably their diet which had caused the issue. If it wasn`t their diet hopefully they would get the message and sort out their problem. Given this appraisal, I developed a method to deliver the news. I would invite them to a meeting in the Personnel Office and say gently, `I`ve have had a complaint about your personal hygiene.....,` then to quickly blurt out `its probably caused by your diet and the food that you eat.`

The positive part of this theory being that by attributing the issue to their diet they would retain a small element of self esteem and tell anyone who cared to ask that they had eaten too much garlic/curry etc. The flip side was those who couldn`t be bothered to wash or wear clean clothes who walked out of the office wondering what their Personnel Manager was on about. Sadly those individuals usually had a nasty surprise in store from their colleagues, usually in the form of cans of deodorant left at their machine.

The good news was that on several occasions my gentle approach did work and it became a reliable and trusted technique in the way of breaking this uncomfortable news. Was it entirely foolproof? Not exactly........!

I recall one case whereby we had employed a local lady for whom English was her first language and who had previously worked at another large local factory. She had worked for her previous employer for 20 years and during the course of the interview she was asked why she now wanted to leave. She replied that she quite liked the work but that during her employment there wasn`t a particularly good atmosphere amongst the workers. Indeed no one showed any friendliness to her and they tended to be very cliquey. We reassured her that our company was different and that the workforce did get on well. She seemed like an ideal candidate for the company.

Within a couple of days of her starting, one of the supervisors appeared at the door of the personnel office. Luckily for me I wasn`t there that day, I was visiting one of the other business units. Unfortunately for Jill my secretary, she *was* there and quickly got on the phone. Now Jill was eager to start taking on a bit more HR work and any opportunity to do so she welcomed with open arms. Jill was aware of how we dealt with such complaints and as I wasn`t back for a number of days, she was keen to deal with the problem. Of course I immediately agreed to her request as Jill was more than capable of delivering the agreed message. When I put the phone down I was confident that the matter would be resolved, if a little relieved that I had managed to get out of delivering the bad news!

Unfortunately things didn`t exactly go according to plan. Within an hour Jill was back on the phone.

`How did it go?` I asked.

`I did it just as we agreed,` replied Jill

`What you sat her down and said that it was probably her diet?` I asked.

`Yes. I did it exactly as we said.`

`Then what happened?` I said.

`She ran out of the office crying,` Jill replied.

`Where did she go?` I said.

`I saw her run out the front door and up the road,` Jill said.

Oh dear, back to the drawing board!

When Jill and I later discussed the matter we recalled the fact that she had worked for a company for twenty years and had said that people were not friendly towards her. On reflection it seemed likely that no-one had ever told her about her problem, until now.

***

The cases of poor personal hygiene kept coming and another involved a lady whom I`d employed in manufacturing. Even the aloof world of HR allows you sometimes to develop a genuine, if professional, affection for some employees and Winnie was such a case in point.

She had moved to the UK from Africa with her children and was very happy when we were able to offer her a job as a machinist. She was the sort of person whose smile would light up a room. Equally she was a hardworking individual and reliable in every way. At her interview she asked whether she could have special leave as she had already booked a holiday back home in Africa and we readily agreed. On her return she very kindly bought me a gift of a lovely hand carved wooden African elephant. Obviously we were normally unable to accept gifts but quite simply it would have broken her heart had I not been able to accept so I found a place for it in my office.

Now even though this was the mid 1980`s, every time Winnie saw me she would curtsey and call me `Sir`. Now believe me I had asked her on numerous occasions to call me by my Christian name and not to curtsey but she seemed to be totally unable to get out of the habit. Now this was not a particular issue if we bumped into each other in the corridor because I would say hello and gently rebuke her for using the term `Sir` and tell her that she did not need to curtsey. It did however become rather embarrassing on occasions when I was showing guests or interviewees around the factory.

Indeed the old Greater London Council used to send inspectors round to their suppliers to check that the suppliers were employing a satisfactory number of women and people from ethnic minorities. Now these inspectors had the power to remove the contract from offending organisations and let me tell you the inspectors were not pleasant people to deal with. My company employed significantly higher numbers of both females and ethnic minorities and in-spite of this fact, we still received harsh treatment from the inspectors, under threat of losing important contracts.

One such visit from the GLC was going relatively smoothly and we were on a tour of the factory and head office. The one person whom I had hoped not to bump into on our tour of the factory was Winnie! Despite my coaching she was totally unable to get out of her old habit and the resulting curtsey and cheery `Hello Sir` from Winnie led her being interviewed by the inspectors and to them giving me an extended grilling about the way that staff were expected to behave.

I seem to have managed to go off at a tangent however let me return to the hygiene issue. I received a visit from a supervisor saying that complaints had been made about Winnie`s personal hygiene. My heart immediately sank as I knew that this job would fall to me. Indeed I didn`t want it to fall to anyone else as I felt that we had a good working relationship and that she may be a bit sensitive to receiving this news. I asked for the supervisor to send Winnie down to see me and sure enough within a minute she appeared at my door.

I had already decided to use the `its probably what you eat` tack as over time this had been least painful for all concerned. Having greeted Winnie and sat her down I said, `Winnie I`m sorry to have to say this but there has been a complaint about your personal hygiene…it`s probably the food that eat…do you eat a lot of curries for example?`

`No` she replied. `I don`t eat curry. I don`t eat spicy food at all`.

I was stumped. Winnie`s eyes started to well up and I offered her a tissue.

She said, `They`ve even complained about my kids at their school. I have to get up at 5am in the morning to wash them before they go to school. The Mayoress came to tea last Sunday and she didn`t complain that we smelled.`

To be honest it was a heartbreaking situation to deliver that sort of news to a genuinely nice person. One can only try to empathise with someone who has been told such news, who then has to return to the workplace to face her colleagues. I gave Winnie the rest of the day off and but sadly she didn`t stay with the company for much longer than a few weeks afterwards.

Personal hygiene wasn`t the only `minging` issue in the workplace. Back in the mid 1980`s companies were not sufficiently switched on to the needs of those religions that did not find it acceptable for their flesh to come into contact with the toilet seat, and my company was no exception.   Generally speaking this was not a problem in the men`s toilets and therefore I had never heard of it. Jill my secretary did however mark my card that at times there were `accidents ` in the ladies toilets when women had been crouching on the seats and had unfortunately missed the target.

 I was somewhat perplexed that Jill knew about this and when I asked her she confirmed that she had once looked under the toilet door and not seen any feet in contact with the ground!

4 STRANGE THINGS THAT HAPPENED TO THIS HR MANAGER

I had been working in manufacturing for some months and it became apparent that my secretary Jill was going to be needed to undertake more hours for the Directors. I therefore needed some dedicated secretarial support, if not to undertake some of my administration and general organisational needs, then to act as the buffer between myself and the wacky work of the employee on the shop floor.

My office was situated right on the shop floor and it was extremely accessible for anyone who wished to `pop in`. Frequently such visits were pleasant and uneventful, however on other occasions it was possible for warring factions to burst in and demand that you acted as some sort of referee. One of the key duties for my secretary was to sit in the area immediately outside my door and tell most of the potential visitors that I was "in a meeting" or "interviewing", or attending to some other equally uninterruptible matter of vital importance.

As well as being a capable typist [in those days], they needed to have the organisational skills of an Olympic planner, the patience of a counsellor and the `diplomacy` of a bouncer.

At that time, employment opportunities in that sort of role were fairly plentiful and occasionally you find candidates who had `embroidered` their qualifications slightly, and were prepared to chance their arm to try to make a career change etc. In other words they had never really spent any time in this sort of work but had lied on their cv and were hoping that they may be the best of a bad bunch.

I was fairly pleased when five suitable candidates responded to the advert and we organised a day of interviews and typing tests. Having been given one page of typing to copy, one of the candidates had six attempts before ripping up the final page of A4 paper and storming out of the building. Until then she had scored well on patience if not on typing ability!

There was however one excellent candidate who met all the criteria and as well as that, had an excellent sense of humour. Joanne was a local girl in her mid-twenties who had made her living from secretarial roles since she left school. I was delighted when we offered her the job and she accepted. A long month then passed as she worked her notice and I was working overtime to get everything done.

In order to give Joanne a good start I had planned an induction. On arrival I would meet her and spend an hour with her to introduce her to the working environment and settle her in gently. I had then arranged for her to spend an hour with the most senior secretary who was responsible for undertaking work for the Directors etc. Following that I would give her a tour of the factory and introduce her to the key employees who she would be likely to see on a regular basis.

Jo arrived on time and we spent a very pleasant hour chatting about the organisation and her role within it. At the end of that I asked her if she would pop down to the senior secretary`s office and then come back in about an hour. In the mean time I was still `snowed under` with work and was hoping for an opportunity to make some progress.

Just after Joanne left me there was a knock at my door and stood there was Rob the Production Controller.

`You couldn`t do me a favour could you?`, Rob said.

Now Rob and I had an excellent working relationship and I was only too pleased to help. `What would you like me to do?`, I replied.

`You're about 36" waist and 31" leg aren't you?` he asked.

`How on earth did you know that?`, I said. `I've been in the business man and boy,` he replied.

Nevertheless I was extremely impressed that he could establish my trouser size so accurately.

`We've just had some trousers come off the line of that size and need someone to try them to see if they fit,` he said, `can you assist?`

`I'm happy to help, but where is there to try them on?` I asked.

Bearing in mind that my office was on the shop floor and had a two feet square pane of glass in it, I felt a bit concerned that my dignity may not by protected if I were to try the trousers on. Rob however reassured me, he said `Look, at this time of day most of the shop floor are working at their machines now, there's not much chance of anyone coming in.`

I thought about it quickly and on reflection he was right. Normally there were a lot of people moving around just before break times but this was only one hour into the working day. I should therefore be fairly safe for a quick change.

Rob left me with the trousers and I promised I would try them on within the next couple of minutes. Without further ado, I dropped my suit trousers to the floor, and got into the inveritable struggle that you inevitably get into when trying too hard to get trousers on and off quickly. Just as I was at the point when the first foot seemed to getting into the trouser leg there was a knock at the door and the simultaneous appearance of my new secretary Jo's head at my window.

Unfortunately she had gone to the senior secretary's office and found that she was not there. Using her common sense she has returned to see me and had indeed seen more than she bargained for! Within an hour of starting her new job she had found her new boss in his office with his trousers around his ankles.

Through the glass I could see her face drop and she quickly scurried off. Goodness knows what the poor girl was thinking and goodness knows where she was going. It wasn`t as if I could quickly rectify the matter. How could anyone give chase with one foot in, and one foot out of a pair of trousers?

It didn`t take too long to get the trousers on and I rushed out to find Jo pacing up and down in the corridor. The blood had drained from her face and she had the look of someone who thought they had just made a very big mistake in leaving their previous employer.

`Jo, it`s not what you think,` I pleaded, `I was just trying to help the production control team.`

Luckily for me and in the nick of time, Rob came bounding up and said ` Well, do they fit? You`re not supposed to walk off in them!`

There was a very uncomfortable few seconds whilst Jo processed what she had just seen. I quickly saw my opportunity to introduce Rob to Jo and it didn`t take her long to burst out laughing. Rob, of course, thought that the whole thing was hysterical and never, ever, shut up about it from that point on.

***

Whilst HR can be a very serious business for much of the time, we did find times for the odd practical joke. On one occasion I recall being on the end of one of Rob`s practical jokes.

Now my telephone would never stop ringing. From speaking to potential employees to dealing with recruitment agencies there was always someone on the line. This fact wasn`t lost on Rob and whilst I was on lunch one day, he filled the base on my telephone with the toner used to refill the photocopier. This was a particularly fine powdery substance which had the sole purpose in life of making anything that it touched very black indeed.

In the early part of the afternoon I had been closeted away in the office fielding numerous calls and been completely oblivious to the fact that every time I put the phone to my ear I was leaving an increasingly large black mark on my ear.

Later that afternoon, when it became necessary to venture onto the shopfloor, I was delighted at how the workforce were greeting me with such lovely smiles. They had clearly forgotten about the occasions when I had to act as the company policeman and rebuke them for their lack of productivity, poor attendance, lateness etc etc. Hey, I could see their affection for me written all over their faces. I wasn`t to know that never before had the workforce seen their Personnel Manager striding amongst them with a completely blackened ear!

Now Rob was able to see the entertainment through his office window and I could see that the poor fellow was doubled up as if he was having an asthma attack. Concerned for his health I popped my head around his door and said `Are you OK mate?`

He was virtually incapable of speaking but I just managed to hear, `I`m OK but I `ear that you`re not,` as he almost fell off his chair laughing, you`re a bit off colour, ha, ha, ha....`.

I looked at him quizzically and he said, `now look `ear, don`t give me one of those black looks,` as the tears were rolling down his cheeks.

I caught site of a mirror in his office, saw my blackened ear and could see that I had been "well and truly had!" There was no point in doing anything other than to laugh along with the joke and resolve to "not get mad, but to get even". I outwardly laughed and inwardly resolved to get even with Rob whenever the opportunity arose.

***

As luck would have, it wasn`t long before I saw my chance. Rob was a creature of habit and would always make his own sandwiches and bring them into work for his lunch. There was only ever one round of sandwiches. They were on brown bread and always wrapped in cling film. Rob must have bought a job lot of brown paper bags because those sandwiches always came in an identical brown bag.

As well as being a bit of a joker, Rob was a very generous individual and on the occasions when he had either worked through lunch or been taken out by a supplier, he would kindly drop his sandwiches in to me. This was very much appreciated by a hungry Personnel Manager.

On Fridays the factory would close at 1pm and we would usually get away early for the weekend. On one such Friday Rob had not had the chance to eat his sandwiches and popped into my office before leaving, wished me a good weekend and kindly left his sandwiches. Now I had already eaten but was particularly enthused and invigorated by the potential for revenge. I decided to leave the sandwiches in the heat of the office for the weekend and on my return on Monday, the sandwiches were covered in mould.

I had no doubt that when Rob came in his sandwiches would be identical to his usual fare and I was not wrong. I awaited my opportunity and when he left his office for a moment, I substituted the mouldy sandwiches for the fresh ones. Quite honestly, the two packages were absolute ringers. Not even Rob would have been able to tell them apart

Determined to see the fruits of my labours, I bought a roll from the canteen and as I sometimes did, dropped into Rob`s office so that we could have a quick `natter` over lunch. He said `Hello mate, I`ve only got time for a quick sarnie as I have to pop out for a minute.`

`Ok`, I said, `Don`t worry I`m in a bit of a rush as well, got a lot on today. We can neck `em and get cracking.`

As ever he was his usual friendly and entertaining self and didn`t even bother to look at his mouldy sandwich before heartily tucking in and telling me about his exploits over the weekend. I listened patiently and made a few non-verbal grunts to encourage him and keep his attention as he managed to talk and scoff down his sandwich at the same time.

I said, `to change the subject, you like a bit of music Rob don`t you? I was trying to remember that hit by Lieutenant Pigeon, I heard it on the radio the other day, what was it called?`

`Oh yes,` he said, `I like my seventies, was it an instrumental?`

`I think so,` I replied, `didn`t it get to number one in the charts?`

`I think it did, ` he said, `was it Mouldy old dough?`

`I think it may have been,` I said, trying to suppress my giggles, `it wasn`t by Bread though was it?`

`No they did the love songs didn`t they,` he replied his face starting to twig that something was making me chuckle a bit too much.

`Was "Mouldy old dough" named after your sandwiches?`, I said.

`What do you mean,` he replied, `these are freshly made today, by my own fair hand, there`s no mould on....`

`If you don`t mind me saying they look a bit past their sell by date,` I said.

He looked down, went as white as a ghost, and for a split second couldn`t compute what was taking place. His surprise was only matched by the hysteria from myself and another colleague who was in on the joke.

`You`ll have to be a bit more careful with that bread mate, it looks a bit stale,` I helpfully advised.

By then it was too late. Rob had swallowed most of it, mould and all! He didn`t know whether to laugh, cry or be sick. On balance he chose the right option which was the last of three and went sprinting off to the gent`s toilets to throw up.

They say that leopards don`t change their spots but I do recall that never again did Rob`s sandwiches appear to be identical to each other, and never again did he play a practical joke on me!

***

From time to time in HR you do get some strange people turning up and asking to see you. On one such occasion the senior secretary Jill phoned me in a bit of a flap to tell me that there was a man in reception asking to see personnel. I asked what the purpose of his visit was and she said that he was a former employee who claimed to be owed some money. I could tell from the flustered tone of her voice that she wanted me to see him. I told her that I would be out to reception in a moment.

When I arrived there was a fairly dishevelled middle aged man clutching a plastic bag, the like of which you would find in a supermarket checkout. Now I was aware that we had some important customers due to arrive and I felt that it would better to see man away from the public reception area. I introduced myself and asked him if he would like to come through to my office. He readily agreed.

There was a walk of around forty yards to the office and during the course of the walk I asked him the purpose of his visit. He replied ` I used to work here and when I left they didn`t pay me my weeks` notice.`

`When did you leave?` I asked, having only been there a few weeks myself.

`About five years ago, and before you ask, I don't have a bomb in this bag.`

Well, had I done so it would have been the first time that I had ever asked a visitor if they were bringing a bomb into the building! I immediately formed the impression that I had invited the local nutter back to the personnel office.

When we got there, he put the bag down and again said `its not a bomb in there.`

I said, `Well you`ve got me intrigued now, what exactly do you have in there?`

`You can take a look,` he said.

With some trepidation I slowly parted the plastic bag and was somewhat relieved to see that the only contents were a couple of lamb chops.

`Well you`ve got your lunch sorted,` I said.

`More tasty than a bomb,` he replied.

Quite frankly all this talk about bombs at this time of the morning was making me a tad nervous so I thought that I would try to bring things to a conclusion as soon as possible.

I said ` Did you ask for the money that you were owed when you left?`

`No`. He replied.

`And have you spoken to anyone about this since?` I asked.

`No?` He replied.

`And you are sure that you`re owed the money?`

`Oh Yes,` he said, with conviction.

This man was distinctly odd and I really didn`t want him around the place. Thinking quickly, I lied `Payroll aren`t in today, they`re all on day off, can you write your name and address down and I`ll look into this first thing tomorrow morning.`

He wrote down his name on a piece of paper followed by the words, "man with no bomb" and I managed to convince him that this would be a priority job for the next day. With that he shambled out into the street. I suspect that he was headed for the next business along the road and was going to try them all until someone coughed up. I did however take the trouble to check his name against the records of previous employees but it did not appear that he had ever worked for the business.

***

Normally work was quite intense in the week and on weekends I used to try to forget about things. Just occasionally however something would happen whereby you were needed to provide some Personnel input on an issue. I recall one classic occasion. It was a Saturday and I was returning home from a game of golf. I lived more than twenty miles from the office so normally I was safe from bumping into employees in the supermarket etc.

The large retail organisation that I worked for used to deliver on Saturday mornings in my area. They had a fleet of vans all of which were liveried and clearly identified as belonging to the company. As the drivers were required to go into customers homes, at the time there was a rule which prohibited the wearing of rings through noses and scruffy appearance etc.

On this Saturday I was a little weary after golf and happened to find myself travelling behind one of our delivery vans as it approached a narrow stretch of road. Normally this road was fairly quiet and only infrequently did you meet a vehicle coming the other way. As we travelled along we suddenly slowed down as I could see a vehicle approaching. It was a driving school vehicle being driven by a young teenage female driver, accompanied by her instructor.

As we got closer it was fairly obvious that there was not sufficient room for the two vehicles to pass. The company van stopped with an apparent invitation for the other vehicle to reverse. Either the young driver wasn`t able to reverse or had been instructed by her teacher to stay put. As a result there was an impasse, and the traffic came to a halt.

At this point I wasn`t overly concerned, after all I`d had a good game of golf and was feeling quite relaxed. I thought it likely that the holdup would sort itself out and that we would shortly be on our way.

Unfortunately I was wrong. I could see that the two vehicles were not far apart and that words seemed to be exchanged between the van driver and the instructor in the other vehicle. The poor young girl was looking quite frightened as she was stuck in the middle between the two warring factions. Rather than one vehicle backing up they slowly moved closer together. By now hand gestures were being made by both sides and I felt that the matter was starting to escalate. All of a sudden, the door of our van opened and a large employee jumped up to confront the driver of the other vehicle.

Now this individual had piercings all over the place and quite honestly looked like the wild man of Borneo. How he had come to be employed by his manager I will never, ever, know. He was physically intimidating and must have been about 6` 2" and weighed about 15-16 stones.

Within a flash he was trying to open the driver's side door of the other vehicle and the both the girl and her relatively small in stature instructor were looking terrified. I realised that I would have no choice but to get involved.

Luckily for me I had my company ID card with my photo saying "Regional Personnel Manager" in my glove compartment. I quickly jumped out and approached the van driver.

` You need to get back in your vehicle.` I said.

'What the fuck has it got to do with you?` he said, looking very aggressively at me, 'what are you going to do about it then?` For a split second he must have felt fairly empowered. After all, he was a big fellow effectively trying to bully and intimidate a young girl and her relatively small teacher, and now some bloke in his golfing gear was telling him to get back in his van!

It was clear to me that he would have worked from a regional delivery depot and I knew his manager Bill Moore quite well having worked with him on various HR matters. I produced my ID card and said ` I'm the Regional Personnel Manager for 80 stores in this area including your depot and I know Bill Moore very well. That's what the fuck it has to do with me, get back in the van NOW!`

For a few, precious fleeting moments, his face was a picture and he didn't even need to speak. Of all the people to have behind you when driving the liveried company van and ready for a bit of "road rage" was the bloody Personnel Manager ! Rather sheepishly he returned to his vehicle.

I can only wonder what the couple in the car thought of the incident. One minute they are under serious threat, the next minute someone dressed as a golfer comes from nowhere, waves a magic card and the wild man returns to his vehicle with his tail between his legs. I have never seen such a grateful look of relief on a pair of faces.

***

In the late 1980's I had gained a new position with a company which I knew involved a significant amount of travel throughout the length and breadth of the UK. There was a regular team meeting each month which involved a journey to the Head Office in the north of the country. The drive took about four hours and involved an overnight stay in an hotel. I was not looking forward to the first meeting as it was in the middle of winter it was certainly not a pleasure.

As my local base was nearer to the Head Office than my home, my plan was to take an overnight night bag and a fresh shirt and socks etc to work and then keep the same suit trousers and jacket for the following day. The suit jacket and fresh shirt would be hung in the back of the car as I made my journey to keep them from creasing for the next day.

On this particularly dark and dismal day in winter it was late and I was tired as I was driving north for the meeting. I was looking forward to getting to the hotel and changing into some casual clothes and having a meal.

At 9pm at night the road was very quiet and I had completed about three quarters of the journey when I approached some road works on the motorway. For a very short distance they had changed the speed limit but the sign was not prominently displayed and obviously I hadn't slowed down enough. My heart sank as suddenly in my mirror I saw the blue light of a police traffic car and realised that it was me that they wanted to stop.

The officer asked me to join him in his vehicle which I duly did and then subsequently I received my rollicking for travelling too fast. I was let off with a caution and quickly made my way back to my car to finish my journey. It was really cold out of the vehicle and in my haste to get back in I managed to catch my shirt pocket on the top of the door. From the noise of the rip I could immediately tell that I had inflicted major damage and sure enough, the pocket was completely ripped to the point where both sides of stitching had gone and what should have been pointing upwards was hanging downwards! My initial annoyance was however tempered by the fact that I had packed my usual fresh shirt and that it shouldn't be too much of a problem.

In my state of weariness I quickly forgot about the incident and eventually arrived at the hotel at 10pm. I was too late for a meal but still able to order room service before doing some preparation for the meeting the following day and turning in for the night.

After a good night`s sleep I arose and had a quick shower before getting dressed. When I went to the wardrobe I located my jacket and expected my fresh shirt to be hanging underneath it. No shirt. My first monthly HR meeting with my new team was starting at 8.30am and there was absolutely no chance of popping out to buy a new shirt.

Trying to remain calm I frantically looked for the previous days shirt. I found it in the bottom of the cupboard where it had been discarded in a heap and it was now completely creased, ripped and decidedly grubby. With time running out I realised that I had no alternative but to iron the shirt and to try to repair it by using the hotel sewing kit, if there was one. My hopes were raised when after a couple of minutes I located the hotel sewing kit. My euphoria was unfortunately short lived when I realised that the only thread available was red which was unlikely to look good against my white shirt!

I never was much good at sewing and I wasn`t too impressed with my efforts to repair my shirt. In a word the white shirt with `u` shaped red stitching around the pocket looked hideous. In fact it not only looked bad it didn`t smell too good either!

In the circumstances my only choice was to wear my buttoned up jacket for the full eight hours of the team meeting. It must have looked that I was about to get up and leave at any time and goodness knows what my new colleagues thought of the latest addition to the HR team. Why was this new person insisting on keeping his jacket on even whilst sweating like a pig?

5 PERSONAL RELATIONSHIPS IN THE WORKPLACE

If there is anyone who does not believe that personal relationships go on at work, they must be living on a different planet. The workplace throws people together for longer in a working day than the time that those people spend with their families when they get home.

There are periods of great stress during which a work colleague can show greater comfort than someone may expect when they get home. It has always been a fertile place for people to meet and it never ceases to amaze me how attractive a fairly bland senior executive can become to a member of the opposite sex.

I recall one five foot four inch balding Chief Executive who was engaged in a relationship with one of his female managerial colleagues. He had not been at the organisation for very long whilst she had been around for many years and had systematically been attracted to those of a more senior position. Secretly he probably thought that he was quite special to have attracted her whilst everyone else knew that he was one of a very long list of conquests. Somehow she had managed to outlast most of them and was incredibly unpopular amongst her female colleagues.

The knowing glances, the unusual meetings without purpose, the pairing on away days, the late evenings...etc, etc. It was a classic case where those individuals involved think that their office romance is a great secret, and in fact it is *their* secret. They are completely oblivious to the fact that the whole of Head Office is talking about it and waiting for the next instalment.

Sometimes the office romance causes ripples which go outside of the workplace. I once worked for a particularly aggressive female HR manager who was feared by many of the managers who came into contact with her. She rightly had a particular hatred of anyone who used their position to try to harass female members of staff. One day I was in my car travelling between offices when she called me in a rage because there was an allegation that a young female staff member, who we'll call Julie, was being sexually harassed by her Assistant Manager.

The stepfather of the girl had telephoned my manager to complain and had also faxed a letter of complaint. I was told to literally stop whatever I was doing and visit the family that evening. That meant an overnight hotel stay for a trip of about 130 miles and a visit to a store en-route to collect a copy of the faxed complaint. I went home to collect a change of clothes and headed up country for an appointment with the girl and her parents at their house prior to visiting the store the following day.

By way of background, Julie had worked for the company since she was 16 years old. She had started as a Saturday girl whilst still at school and worked on weekends. Gradually she had increased her hours and when school finished she became full time. At the time of my visit she had worked for the company for around 3 years and was now in a sales role.

I arrived at the smart semi-detached house in middle England at around 8pm, to be greeted by Julie's parents. They were somewhat 'stony faced' but politely showed me into their lounge. They sat protectively on either side of Julie with the young lady somewhat sandwiched in the middle.

Prior to arriving I had parked the car and read the contents of the stepfather's letter. The complaints were levelled at one member of staff, the Assistant Manager of the store who I'll call 'Mark Willis'. He was quite a young man and was only 5-6 years older than Julie. The complaints could be categorised as follows:

1] She was being sexually pestered by the Assistant Manager Mark Willis.

2] Mr Willis had refused to recommend her for a pay rise unless she entered a sexual relationship with him.

3] She was made to undertake cleaning duties in the store after all other members of staff had left at times when only she and the assistant manager were present and this was not part of her job description. Indeed her stepfather corroborated the fact that when collecting her from work, he would often have to wait outside in the car for 20 minutes whilst she was made to sweep up.

4] Mr Willis had a habit of making comments of a sexual nature about her breasts.

By way of gently settling Julie prior to getting onto the complaint itself we initially discussed her employment with the company over the previous three years. She confirmed that she was very contented in her sales role and that whilst she was unhappy with the behaviour of the assistant manager, she actually hadn`t wanted to make a formal complaint herself. It was in fact, her stepfather who insisted in making the complaint.

During the course of our discussion her parents would interject and her stepfather said that she had become very miserable and tearful over recent weeks and that was why they had a `heart to heart` discussion with her. In the course of this discussion she had broken down and told them the story about the behaviour of the assistant manager. Her mother mentioned that Julie had a boyfriend for the last two years, that the family were very fond of him and that he would have killed Mark Willis had he known what he was doing.

I went on to explain that I had a duty to investigate both sides of the complaint and that I would need to have to have specific incidents including dates and times so that I could put them to Mr Willis. Julie was particularly vague about any specific incidents, almost to the point whereby she was deliberately trying not to give me anything to put to him. In fact after half an hour I seemed to have a letter of complaint from the stepfather but little or nothing from the girl herself.

I decided to try a different tack and explained that I was always impartial in all such investigations and that I would need to clarify whether there had ever been any form of consensual relationship between the two of them.

I said to Julie `Did you and Mark ever have a relationship other than a working relationship?`

`Not really` she said

At this point I could sense that her parent`s demeanour changed slightly. "Not really" in my experience did not quite equate to "No".

I said, `For example were you ever boyfriend and girlfriend?`

`Err, no,` she unconvincingly replied

I said, `Did you ever go out socially together, on dates for example?`

After a nervous pause she said, `Well we did go out in his car once and sat by the river.`

`Was that just the two of you or was anyone else there,` I said.

`Just the two of us,` she said.

I said `Is there any suggestion that he forced you to go out with him?`

`No,` she said.

`That`s news to us,` said the stepfather.

I replied, `Given the nature of the very serious allegations in the letter, do forgive me for asking you a very personal question, but did anything of a sexual nature happen when you went out with Mark Willis?`

She said `We sat in the car by the river........and.......stripped off...but nothing happened.`

At this point there was a collective intake of breath from her parents as their heads turned inwardly to look at their 18 year old daughter sitting between them.

I said ` Why would you do that if you had no relationship with him?`

She made no answer but looked at the ground.

A relatively short time thereafter our interview was concluded. She had been unable to provide me with any specific incidents where she had been sexually harassed. It was not long after arriving at my hotel room that I received a telephone call from Julie. She explained that in the previous few weeks she had been upset and that when her parents had questioned her as to why, she had given them half a story about the assistant manager. Enraged her stepfather had written the letter of complaint triggering the investigation.

She confirmed that she had been involved in a relationship with the assistant manager, even though she had a boyfriend and he was engaged to be married. The relationship had subsequently broken up and that had been very painful and upsetting. She asked me if she could withdraw the complaint.

The following day I paid a visit to the store. It was in the sort of location where they rarely received any visitors from a member of the regional management team, particularly at 9am in the morning when they were opening their doors to the public.

Fortunately it was the day off for the manager and I was met by a very surprised Mark Willis, Assistant Manager. After introducing myself we decamped to the manager`s office and I explained the reason for my visit. Visibly shaken he readily admitted that he and Julie had embarked upon an affair for the past 18 months and that the affair had ended when she asked him to break off his engagement to his long term girlfriend. He refused to do as she asked so Julie became very upset, a fact which was very apparent to her parents. It was very clear that there had been no harassment whatsoever and that anything that had happened was consensual.

I returned to my office and informed to my manager. She seemed mildly disappointed at the news and I was left with the feeling that she had been baying for blood and looking for a scalp.

***

Another example of how relationships at work can end in tears occurred at the Head Office of one of the companies that I worked for. In those days companies used to run training schemes for young people who had recently left school. Typically they would spend 1-2 years with the company and during that time receive training to undertake employment in the commercial world. Very often the trainee was employed by the company at the end of their training.

Generally speaking someone from within HR was nominated to run the training scheme and they would act at a focal point for the trainee and management to try to maximise the benefits for both trainee and the company.

The company that I worked for at the time treated this particular scheme with some importance and therefore put one of its most highly regarded Training Managers, who I`ll call Gary McKeown, in charge of the scheme. Gary was the sort of person who was really going places. Now in his mid-thirties he had risen up through the ranks and become professionally qualified along the way. He could cope with any challenge that was thrown at him and certainly gave the scheme some credibility with the senior operations management within the business.

Gary would work very long hours and was based within the company head office. This brings me to a pet hate of mine. Some people, particularly those based within a head office, would try to portray that they worked extremely long hours, even when they didn`t. When buying a suit for work, one particular trick was to buy two jackets and one pair of trousers [rather than the other way round] so that the extra jacket could be left on the back of the office chair even when the individual had left for the evening. This tactic was deployed just in case any Directors were walking round late in the day. Now I don`t know if Gary was prone to practice this method however it did have relevance to his case.

Quite often in amongst the annual intake of trainees were relatives of company employees. In this particular year one of the Directors had arranged for his 16 year old daughter Melissa to join the scheme and she was therefore one of 20-30 young people to be managed by Gary

McKeown. Apparently the scheme was progressing well with the youngsters enjoying their training and the company expecting to produce some very worthwhile future staff members.

A management training issue had arisen in my region as this subject was also covered by Gary, I thought that I would take the opportunity of speaking to Gary whilst I happened to be visiting head office. On arriving at his office I could see that whilst his jacket was on the back of his chair he was nowhere to be found. I waited around for some minutes and asked a couple of people but nobody seemed to know where he was.

As time was limited I decided that I would speak to him on the telephone on my return. The following day I telephoned and there was no response. This continued for a couple of days and eventually someone from HR informed me that he had left the company. Well now that was a surprise! One minute his jacket is on his chair, the next he is nowhere to be seen and has left the company. It didn`t seem right. Normally he would given at least one month`s notice if he had left the company.

Inevitably rumours started to circulate, one was that he had been sacked for bootlegging training videos, another that he had just had enough and walked out. Neither of these theories made any sense. For any potential dismissal such as in the bootlegging case he would have been suspended and the matter would have taken a few weeks to conclude. I doubted that he had merely walked out as he was one of those people destined for great things and only a good offer from another company would have prized him away.

Like many a news story it gradually fizzled out and it was a full twelve months later that I actually found out what had happened. Apparently our high flying training manager aged in his mid-thirties had been caught in a compromising position in a storage cupboard with the sixteen year old daughter of a company director. I had it on good authority that this particular `compromising position` did not leave any room for doubt or hastily contrived excuses.

As a result all standard protocol regarding disciplinary procedure had been shelved and he had been dealt with so speedily that he didn`t even have the time to collect his jacket on the way out. Last I hear he was working as a labourer and with very little chance of a return to HR, particularly as someone responsible for the trainee scheme!

***

There were occasions when matters occurring in an employee's private life spilled over into their work life. Sometimes this was by accident, sometimes by design, and sometimes I could only guess at why.

During my time at one company we were employing a gentleman in his early sixties in a driving role. He was sort of fellow who was a typical `Grandad` figure, very friendly and kindly to everyone that he came into contact with. He was a totally reliable employee whom had never had a day off sick, one of the "old school".

At this organisation the company receptionist was tasked with opening all of the post and distributing it to the appropriate individual or department. Early one morning there was a tap on my office door and the receptionist was standing there looking a little shocked and holding a letter.

`What do you think I should do with this?` she asked, handing me the letter.

It was a letter from a lady purporting to be the mistress of the driver. In the days before mobile phones she had no way of contacting him and had no idea that the letter would be opened by someone at his workplace rather than him. It was a letter in which she had poured out her heart and was asking him to finally leave his wife after some years of their affair.

If there was one person who I would not have thought was capable of having an affair it was him and to hear this was quite shocking. It was however not a work related matter so on reflection we decided to reseal the envelope, deliver it to him and not mention it to anyone at all.

***

Company conferences always offered the opportunity for staff to let off steam. Normally they involved both an overnight stay and considerable amounts of alcohol which sometimes led people to over step the mark and take a working relationship with a colleague to another level. Sometimes these things led to a meaningful relationship but more often than not there were red faces in the morning and deep embarrassment for those involved. Often the ripples were felt for many months after the event and some had the potential to last for the rest of their career!

Working in HR, I was always careful to ensure that I was "whiter than white" and could never be accused of not setting a good example. I recall one conference when there several hundred branch managers together in a very large hotel. The day's presentations had finished early and as it had been a successful year, the staff were then able to have a drink at the free bar prior to the evening programme.

I had only been with the company for about 6-7 months and I had been allocated a room on one of the higher floors of the hotel near to where the Directors were staying. As the evening wore I made every effort to speak to as many managers as possible, many of whom I hadn't met before.

In my near vicinity I noticed one of the managers by the name of Lola, enjoying a drink. She was fairly memorable as she was wearing a tight lycra dress and had certainly been attracting the attention of quite a few of the male managers. The drinking had started at about 4pm in the afternoon and in spite of a short break for a meal, had carried on until well after midnight, in fact it was nearer to 3am.

I had been careful to ensure that I hadn't drunk to excess and decided to turn in at about 3am. I was sat on my bed at about 3.15am when I heard a tap on my door. In view of the fact that I was on the top floor of the hotel there is no way that anyone would have had my room number unless they had either followed me or bribed a member of hotel staff.

I was very aware that I was near to the Directors and that I had only been employed by the company for a matter of months. I opened the door to find the lycra clad Lola standing there, slightly the worse for wear saying, 'let me in.'

I said 'No, you can't come in.'

She looked a little shocked.

`Oh go on....` she said... `let me in.`

`No`, I replied, `you`re not coming in, goodnight,` and shut the door.

I sat back down on the bed and there was another tap on the door, then another. Mindful of all of the board of directors being awoken, I again opened the door and very firmly told her that I was not interested and that she should return to her room. That was the last tap on the door. I later heard that the talk at the breakfast table was not of who had paired off but that this particular person had been `brushed off`!

My professionalism stood me in good stead a matter of months later as Lola was dismissed for work performance related issues. In view of the fact that sometimes I was present at appeals against dismissal, imagine if I upheld the decision to dismiss her and she told me that actually my performance wasn`t up to much either!

Luckily that did not happen but what I did receive was a telephone call from her solicitor trying to negotiate a financial settlement upon her leaving. I wasn`t compromised and she didn`t get the pay off!

***

There were times when relationships at work would get very complicated indeed. One of the companies that I worked for had two business units which were located about 90 miles apart. In the Bristol office the Manager Jim Smith was in a settled relationship with a colleague named Kelly who worked as an administrator. Because she did not report directly to him, it was acceptable for them to work in the same building under the HR policy of the company. They were committed to each other, at least on the face of it, and due to sign for a mortgage on a property within days.

In Birmingham in unit B, Rob Southwell worked as the Assistant Manager who through the needs of the business was often speaking to Kelly from Bristol. Even though they had never met, over time they formed an attachment over the telephone and even though they each had partners, arranged to secretly meet on their day off.

Rob Southwell`s fiancé Miriam, was the only one of the three who did not work for the company and in fact at eight months pregnant, was looking forward to the birth of their first child.

Now Rob was obviously not good at hiding his deceit from his fiancé and later that evening she found out about him spending his day off with Kelly. Being a woman scorned, she decided to make an early morning 90 mile trip to Bristol to confront Kelly her love rival.

She arrived at reception and asked to see Kelly. Not expecting a visit, Kelly thought that she was going to reception to meet a customer. What she found was a heavily pregnant woman screaming the building down and threatening to kill her. Not surprisingly the receptionist was a little out of her depth and decided to call the unit manager Jim to come down to reception to calm the situation. Jim subsequently arrived at reception to find a now hysterical heavily pregnant Miriam alleging that one of his staff was conducting a relationship with her husband Rob, who was also employed by the company in Birmingham.

It didn`t take Jim long to work out that it was his own partner Kelly who was alleged to be seeing Miriam`s husband which didn`t exactly assist in calming the troubled waters! It was a matter of great fortune that a security manager was visiting the unit and able to prevent bloodshed. I never did find out whether either couple had stayed together however it was a classic example of personal issues spilling over into working life.

**

Sometimes in the workplace things are not quite as they seem. I recall one occasion when I had recently joined a company I was visiting an engineering department. As the manager showed me around the department we passed a desk in an area where the supervisors sat. At the time all of the supervisors were out working so no one was present but I noticed that one of the desks was adorned with pictures of young topless models.

This was the sort of thing that you saw in garage workshops in the 1970`s but by the late 1990`s/2000`s they really were a thing of the past in a professional business. Furthermore they had the potential of being cited in any sexual discrimination claim. I didn`t say anything at time but clocked it and planned to bring it up when the manager and I had a chance for a chat in the office.

When the opportunity arose I told him what I`d seen and that there were significant risks to the business reputation and finances if they were allowed to remain on view.

I said `I`m assuming that the person responsible is a supervisor and you need to have a word with him today and get them removed straight away.`

He replied, somewhat carefully, `It is a supervisor, and I have previously had a word but *she* refuses to take them down. None of the blokes seem to complain.`

I must admit that I was a little surprised however they were removed later that day.

***

One of my colleagues was dealing with a disciplinary matter with a manager. He was a married man who managed a store where perhaps 15-20 people were employed. He had conducted affairs with 2-3 female members of staff which totally compromised his position as manager and led to claims of favouritism from other staff members as well as suggestions that certain people were over looked for promotion pay rises etc in lieu of those that were `favourites`.

He was summoned to a disciplinary hearing for his poor performance as a manager and at the hearing he `put his hands up` to the fact that his marriage was in trouble and that he had made the terrible mistake of having these affairs with work colleagues. He stated that his wife knew all about his misdemeanours but was prepared to stand by him so that they could work on their marriage. Apart from the above, other important factors relating to his work performance were solid and the store was profitable with good sales figures and low stock loss etc.

A decision was made to issue him with a final written warning and to move him to a new store rather than to dismiss him. Subsequently a letter was produced confirming the allegation, what he had said in his defence and the result of the hearing. On the basis that his wife knew about the matter it was sent to his home address where the first person to open and read it was his wife. She had no knowledge of his philandering at work and the subsequent tremors could be felt for miles around. Never again was such a letter sent in the post they were always delivered to the individual by hand.

6 THEFT, FIDDLES AND DISCIPLINARIES

In twenty years of being an HR Manager I dealt with most issues of staff theft, fiddles and disciplinaries. That said, just when I thought I had dealt with everything, someone would think of a new fiddle! In this chapter I'll give you a flavour of some of the fraudulent things that went on in the workplace.

Massaging mileage expenses is one of the oldest staff fiddles going. Let's face it, numerous employees will add a few miles here and there to gain that little extra in their expenses payment. There is however always one individual who pushes this fiddle too far.

I dealt with one person who was travelling about 90 miles each way to get to and from work in Birmingham. His claim over a two week period should have amounted to about 1,800 miles. Instead, he put in a claim for 8,000 miles! He physically would not have had the time to drive that far in two weeks if he'd driven in a straight line with no stops. What on earth was he thinking about? Did he seriously think that our expenses claims staff were not capable of working out the distance?

***

I also recall a case where an experienced store manager had a bit of a mid-life crisis which got him into big trouble. This particular individual had a nice little job as manager of a store in a provincial town. There was little competition in the town and his store always turned in excellent figures for the key indicators such as sales and stock control.

Over the years I had a number of dealings with this manager and held him in high regard as someone who was competent and professional. When the security and audit departments informed me that his store was showing excessively high stock loss I was surprised to say the least. It transpired that as well as stock loss there were a disproportionate number of refunds issued compared with stores of a similar turnover.

The security department installed some covert cameras and very quickly established that at the time when refunds were being issued there was no customer in the store. It also became clear from the investigation that he had embarked upon an extra-marital relationship with his store administrator.

When interviewed and presented with the facts he readily admitted that he had been having an affair with administrator. Apparently his wife exercised complete control over the family finances and in order to wine and dine his lover he had taken to issuing refunds to non-existent customers totalling thousands of pounds. As a result fourteen years service with the company went down the drain.

***

Another well known fraudsters trick in the retail industry was known as `teeming and lading`. This would normally occur when the person responsible for banking the takings would `borrow` some of those takings and then make up the amount from the takings from the following day.

Some of these cases were because of an obvious criminal theft whereby the perpetrator carefully timed it so they could disappear with as much money as possible. In many other cases it occurred when the cashier had, in their own mind, borrowed the money to pay a bill with the intention of paying it back. The pay back day, for one reason or another never happened and they were constantly `teeming and lading` and borrowing from Peter to pay Paul. Whichever way the employee thought of their actions the company regarded it as a serious breach of procedure and as a misappropriation of funds.

Inevitably it resulted in dismissal for gross misconduct.

I recall one occasion in a busy store when the administrator had `teemed and ladled` to such an extent that she had £35,000 at home. When questioned she volunteered to go straight home and bring the money in!

***

When senior employees were in possession of a corporate credit card you would think that they would be earning enough money not to need to bend the rules too much. Not so. One individual was planning their wedding and used the company credit card to pay for the whole event! Not a great start to married life when you have just been dismissed from your job.

***

It never ceases to amaze me that even senior members of staff such as board members would have their little fiddles. One of the directors at a major company used to buy his cigarettes out of the petty cash. If a staff member had done the same they would have been fired. It goes to show that the more that you have the more that you want, particularly without paying for it!

***

Another little ruse in the retail industry involved managers misappropriating goods to "test" them at home. They were not allowed to do this without written permission of the area manager but what would happen would be that they would borrow an item such as a TV, and use it at home to "test". Weeks would turn into months and during that time audits in their store would have occurred and quite often the goods would be written off as stock loss. After time had moved on the object was just one of many that was written off and remained in the home of the individual.

I do recall dealing with one manager early in my career who had taken an expensive TV to "test"/use at his home. During the course of him borrowing the TV the audit team paid a surprise visit to his store and turned it upside down. The TV was one of the items missing.

As the investigation unfolded the item was miraculously returned to the store during the course of the night and placed in a position which audit had already doubled checked. No prizes for guessing who featured on the cctv and alarm records making a nocturnal visit with the TV.

***

My introduction to workplace theft started very early in fact at a time when I was a trainee with a company who were involved in moving around large amounts of cash. In those days the systems were fairly antiquated and it was not always apparent that bags of cash were missing until the next day.

On this occasion an experienced two man crew were asked to take out a trainee for his first operational experience. They collected seven bags of cash from a bank but only six were delivered to the company vault. The seventh bag containing about £6,000 seemingly disappeared.

As a trainee I was not part of the decision making process but the company undertook a full investigation and was unable to prove who had taken the bag. In addition in those days the company had a strong union presence supporting the employees and was keen to ensure that innocent employees would not be dismissed.

I was fairly sure that the new employee had been set up and that one or both of the more experienced crew had taken the bag but this theory was not provable. As a result no employees were dismissed because of the union issue and the concern that the company would lose at Industrial Tribunal and incur further costs. Someone had got away with the perfect crime.

In the following years UK employment case law changed to allow an employer to fairly dismiss all three employees in a similar situation, despite the fact that two would probably have been innocent.

***

In the retail industry cash handling and banking is a vital part of the job. In my experience of covering hundreds of stores, every so often the day`s takings would disappear. In the time before cctv you were presented with a few scenarios whereby this could happen.

I dealt with situations where the cash had been left on the table of the manager`s office whilst they went to deal with a customer and when they returned it was gone. I also recall cash being left out in the office overnight whilst the manager had locked up and gone home. I have no doubt that some of these situations were down to the manager being opportunistic and trying to claim that whilst they had made a mistake, they hadn`t taken the money themselves. Equally I am sure that on other occasions members of staff or the public had seen an opportunity and taken it. Either way, for a manager the result was usually the same, dismissal for gross negligence.

***

Other fiddles would occur when employees used the company customer base to line their pockets. I recall an engineer who in the course of visiting company customers would tell them that he would return in his own time and fix a problem much more cheaply for cash. He had probably been making quite a bit of cash until the point when one of his repairs had gone wrong and the customer complained to the company. His "on the side" fiddle resulted in the end of his main earning stream!

***

Another employee who was engaged as an engineer developed a drug problem and became desperate for money for his next fix. At his lowest point he would visit a customer to make a repair and then promise to sell them a `super-duper` smart card for which was capable of bringing them just about every TV channel in the world + the fastest possible broadband for free for the rest of their lives. Several paid him the cash and of course he never returned.

His fiddle was not so smart after all when he left them his company mobile phone number in his own handwriting on a piece of paper. On his arrival at my office the first thing that I asked him to do was to write out his mobile number three times on a piece of paper. It was identical to that left with the customer and he had no alternative but to admit to what he had done. Not surprisingly his employment was terminated.

***

For a number of years I worked in a retail environment whereby staff often sold high value items. Many weekend employees were young and in most cases had no chance of affording the sorts of items which they regularly sold. From time to time there would be searches of staff as they were leaving the store. Sometimes this task would be down to the manager who would stand by the door and ask the employee to draw a coloured ball from a bag of balls. If they drew a red ball they would be searched.

Some stores were not efficient at doing this and the process would lapse from time to time before a rollicking to the management and a subsequent surprise search of staff. This was the case in one store and on seeing the manager searching people one young man decided to dump his ill gotten gains of a couple of DVD`s in the canteen. In doing so he had removed them from the same pocket that he had put his payslip in just minutes before and the resulting managerial find was two DVD`s sandwiching his payslip! He was destined for a disciplinary and early removal from the company.

***

The disciplinary hearing is a something which any self respecting HR Manager will be very familiar with. It is definitely an area in which you need to `gain your stripes` and be able to provide the line manger with expert input. No one really wants disciplinary hearings in their company as they are extremely time consuming unproductive affairs. They are however a necessary evil and an opportunity for the company to correct and improve the performance of their employees.

Of course each disciplinary must be handled correctly. Firstly this is to ensure that employees are treated fairly, secondly because otherwise the door is left open for an employment tribunal claim which will be even more time consuming and potentially costly in terms of hard cash and bad publicity.

Before each disciplinary hearing you should conduct a fair investigation to identify the facts of the matter and to give the employee the opportunity of answering allegations before a full blown hearing. They must then be given fair notice of the hearing and normally the right to be accompanied by a colleague or Trade Union Rep. Following the hearing there is a normally right of appeal to the next higher level of management. In my career I worked on probably hundreds of cases for a massive variety of issues, some small and some larger and more serious.

In the workplace you do sometimes get people trying incredibly stupid things to attempt to get a big pay off. One of the ways to do it is to claim that you were injured in a workplace accident in the knowledge that the company was insured and that you could make a personal injury claim. One of the most idiotic cases that I worked on involved an employee who I'll call Dick Merrick. Now Dick was employed in an engineering position which meant that he was quite well paid in a very stable job. He would travel around in his company vehicle making various repairs to a variety of products.

On one Monday morning Dick was in the back of his vehicle preparing to use a piece of equipment which was heavy and tied to the body of the vehicle via secure straps. He claimed that in doing so the strapping was faulty and broke causing a major injury to his shoulder. He subsequently entered the injury in the accident book at work and the following day on the Tuesday, Dick phoned in sick and self-certified his sickness absence. After seven days, in order to qualify for company sick pay, Dick went to his doctor and was signed off sick due to his "shoulder injury". He then remained off work for a number of weeks.

Sometime later the company received a telephone call saying that he was not telling the truth about this incident. The allegation was that he had injured his shoulder on the previous Saturday as the result of a fight at a night club undertaking his part-time role as night club doorman. They further stated that he had attended the hospital Accident and Emergency department. If this was true there was an issue of fraud as well as falsifying the accident book. Both of which would result in his dismissal if proven.

As we were now dealing potentially with a fraudulent claim against the company insurers amounting to over £200,000, the security department was called in. They managed to get hold of the written hospital A and E record which stated that he had been treated on the Saturday night for wrenching injuries to his shoulder following a fight in the nightclub. This record corroborated what we had been told in the telephone call.

So simply lying about his "accident" at work had now started to rapidly escalate and get out of control. Trying to defraud the insurance company of hundreds of thousands of pounds could have resulted in his criminal conviction resulting in a prison sentence. Having worked on many cases of fraud it was obvious to me that his was a false claim and that he was desperately in need of something to bolster his case, for example evidence with a `WOW` factor.

Several months later and out of the blue, I received something which surprised even me. In the course of a number of legal documents arriving from his solicitor, it was a copy of a page of medical notes from his doctor's surgery relating to him which seemed to support his case. The notes listed an appointment at his doctor's surgery several days after his injury where he had referred to the injury which was caused at work by company equipment failing and causing a wrenching injury to his shoulder. This was the first time that he had produced official proof of medical records seeming to link the "work injury" to a visit to his doctor in the days following the alleged accident. The A and E records only detailed a shoulder injury resulting from the night club fight.

I was not at all happy with this document as I had a major problem with his credibility. I therefore wrote directly to his surgery and obtained all of his records and sat down to look at them. We were not sent a copy of the document that had been produced by his solicitor even though we were sent a number of other documents where the handwriting looked very similar. I further checked the dates on the "new" medical notes and it appeared that he had visited his GP on a Sunday. We checked with the practice and of course they never opened on a Sunday. The alarm bells started to ring.

By now the security department was involved and due to the high potential stakes, we decided to get the medical notes examined by a document expert. In my experience this was the only that this had happened during my career because the cost of obtaining a report was very high.

After a couple of weeks we received the report from our expert. It told us in no uncertain terms that the additional page of medical notes was a falsification and a 100% composite of other medical notes relating to him. Effectively what he done was to use software to copy paragraphs and lines from his medical notes and then merge them into a new document which supported his case. We also found out that his wife worked at another local surgery and would have been able to obtain the blank document required onto which he could copy the information. He fell down because the date which he had copied and used as a date which he had seen his GP, related to a Sunday. This could not be true.

Further checks on this individual showed that he must have had something to hide in his past although we were never able to work out exactly what it was. At one point several years before he had changed his name by deed poll from Dick `Merick` to Dick `Merrick`. In my experience this was very unusual but would only have been done to conceal something.

At his subsequent disciplinary hearing Dick continued to claim that his story regarding his injury was corrected in spite of overwhelming evidence against him. He was duly dismissed for gross misconduct and although he appealed, the original decision to dismiss was upheld.

***

Another slightly unusual disciplinary case involved a woman scorned. Karen worked in our customer service department and as a result had access to many customer records. Unfortunately Karen`s partner left her to live with another woman.

In a fit of rage Karen had then checked the company database and found that her love rival was a customer. She then used the details to make nuisance telephone calls and send taxi`s and pizza`s and anything else that she could think of! I`m sure that the resultant disciplinary was somewhat of a nuisance to Karen!

***

Every now and then an employee would fall foul of drink driving legislation and this could have serious implications for their employment. In one company that I worked for the engineers were allowed to use their liveried vehicles in their personal time. That is to say that they could use it to collect the groceries or take the kids to school. They still however had to be mindful that they could not break any road traffic laws or bring the company into disrepute by driving badly or whilst under the influence.

Unbeknown to the company one employee who I'll call Anthony James, had developed a drink problem but he had managed to keep it from his family and work colleagues. One weekend he had been to the pub and had foolishly decided to drive home even though he was well over the legal limit to drive. As he neared his home he lost control and veered off the road and knocked over several fence posts in three gardens before coming to rest in a fourth garden.

As he came to rest he apparently turned towards the house owner and looked at them for a couple of seconds. They could see his face and could plainly see the van with a large company logo on the side. They also recognised him as someone who lived around the corner. Rather than to face up to the problem and the trail of destruction that he had left in his wake, he reversed the vehicle and drove off.

The police subsequently arrived at the scene and called at Anthony James' house with the intention of breathalysing him. The house was in darkness and they received no answer. They elected not to force entry and so Anthony never did receive a breath test and was not banned from driving. He had however brought the company into disrepute and caused damage to property etc. When interviewed he claimed that the vehicle had been stolen in spite of the fact that a couple of residents recognised him as the driver of the vehicle.

I was present at his disciplinary with his manager. These can be quite tense affairs because potentially the company has the ability to dismiss the individual and take away their livelihood. Anthony James was about 6` 4` tall and due to his drinking likely to be a little unstable. We were also aware from his medical record that he had a health problem with his kidney, most likely due to his excessive drinking.

I was aware that his manager had a serious interest in martial arts having previously discussed the subject with him. Likewise I too had previously competed to a reasonable level in martial arts and won a few titles. This always helped in the confidence stakes if matters got a little "difficult".

We went through the disciplinary hearing with James, putting the facts to him and giving him the opportunity to comment. His defence was that his van had been stolen even though he had been seen driving it away from the pub and recognised when it had come to rest in the garden. Furthermore it had been `dumped` about 50 yards from his house. His version of events was just not believable.

The meeting was adjourned to consider a verdict and on his return to the room he was informed that he was to be dismissed for gross misconduct. He immediately jumped up and said, `Right I`ll take you both on then.` We were in an upstairs office in a building with no reinforcements nearby. In front of us we have a large fellow with a drink problem who has just been dismissed and is not happy.

Now I don`t go to work to be a punch bag and equally I have no intention of being anything other than professional with employees. I did however for a fleeting moment contemplate that I may have to defend myself in this situation if I could not talk my way out of it. I also had the advantage of having his medical record in front of me and knowing exactly where he was weak.

His threat to take us was met with an unflinching, unblinking response from us. I suggested to him that he did not make matters worse for himself and in any case he could appeal the decision and that another manager may see it differently.

Luckily for all, after a brief standoff he collected his coat and left. His appeal was unsuccessful.

***

Whilst serious some disciplinary hearings had an almost farcical feel to them. One that I attended with the Regional Manager involved an appeal hearing where a Branch Manager had basically fiddled the petty cash from his branch and been dismissed. Unless he pulled several rabbits out of the hat it was likely that his dismissal would be upheld. This particular branch was in a town in which it was difficult to park but we managed to find a place and arrived in good time.

We went through the process, heard his grounds for appeal and adjourned to consider the verdict. The decision was to uphold his dismissal which he seemed to be expecting as he made the comment `I expect that you`ve parked on double yellow lines haven`t you?` Ooooh, a little unfair I think?!

It was not unusual in the circumstances for the individual to want to remove their personal effects from the office having been dismissed.. After a couple of moments of reflection the manager said `I have a few things that I need to take with me, is it OK if I get them?`

`Yes where are they?` the Regional Manager replied.

`In the basement,` said the manager.

`OK we`ll come down with you while you get them, what are they?`

`It`s a bathroom suite` he replied,

`Are you serious`? replied the Regional Manager

`Yes,` he said, `it`s the toilet, sink and bath, I was keeping them here for a while.`

It is fair to say that we were rendered speechless by this request. The manager was keeping his bathroom suite in his small branch office! We delegated one of the fit young local employees to give him a hand up the stairs with it and he duly left, suite in hand!

***

It never ceases to amaze me how callous and moronic certain human beings can be. In the whole of this book I have been careful not to use the actual names of those involved to keep a veil of confidentiality whilst telling the true story. I want to be particularly careful here as it involves a tragic event.

In a national company employing thousands of staff you will inevitably see tragedy occurring to someone within the business on rare occasions. One of our long serving employees was a particularly valued member of staff. He was a thoroughly decent man employed in a managerial role and with whom I had a few dealings over the years, for routine matters such as recruitment etc. He had a teenage son who by all accounts was a gifted individual and a wonderful son.

Unfortunately his son found himself in the wrong place at the wrong time. He happened to be in a retail unit which was targeted by robbers. During the course of the robbery he was murdered by the criminals, probably because he was a potential witness to what had occurred. The event had a devastating effect on his family and friends and his father, our employee, was given as much time as he needed to cope with his loss before returning to work.

After a couple of months he clearly needed to return to some normality and he asked to return to his work. Some weeks went by and we were pleased at the way he was settling back in to his role. One of his staff worked in the stores department and was a fairly fiery individual. On the day in question they had exchanged words over an issue and the storeman grabbed him by the throat and held him against the wall and threatened him.

When I was made aware of the situation the storeman was immediately suspended and an investigation launched into the facts of the matter. Having received the results of the investigation it was obvious that there was a disciplinary case to answer and this was duly arranged. I decided to attend as it was very important that this case was dealt with `by the book`.

The allegation was that he had assaulted his line manager by grabbing him by the throat and holding him against the wall was put to him. The only response that he could give was that they had an argument over a task in the stores and that he had lost his temper. The task that he had been asked to do was within his job description and capabilities it just appeared that he didn`t want to do it and had lost control.

I said to him `Are you aware of the situation that your manager had recently had to cope with his son murdered during a robbery?`

He replied `Yes`

I said `Do you not think that you should have afforded him more consideration than by grabbing him by the throat following a disagreement?`

He replied `Well it`s not just him, I`ve been through hard times as well, I`ve been divorced.`

I was left shocked and speechless by this total and utter moron. He was duly dismissed.

7 HR MANAGERS AND COLLEAGUES

One of the difficult issues to deal with in Human Resources is when you are tasked with making people redundant. Typically you have a degree of forewarning about this scenario and a little time to plan how it will take effect. If you are going through a significant re-sizing of a company it can take a couple of years before there is a degree of stability.

Whilst redundancy is never easy, there is a silver lining if you are keen to leave the business yourself and hopeful of getting a reasonable pay off. Indeed when you are responsible for a sizable redundancy programme you are usually privy to information which is very explosive indeed for all sorts of reasons ranging from the company share price to the ability of certain key individuals to cause havoc if they realised that they were about to lose their jobs.

On one occasion I was keen to leave an organisation because I was fed up of travelling hundreds of each week and living out of a suitcase. I was therefore able to engineer and negotiate a situation whereby I could effectively make my own position redundant and have a significant amount of time to plan for my own future.

I had made the decision to start my own business and in order to do so, I had decided to give notice on my expensive flat and to move in as a lodger with another of my HR managerial colleagues for 5-6 months before securing redundancy. I therefore moved in with a good friend of mine by the name of `Billy` who kindly let me have a room in his house at very reasonable rates. Billy was a Training Manager at the company and we enjoyed a pint together from time to time.

The arrangement worked really well with my expenses being significantly reduced and it gave me the chance to plan for my new venture. Having Billy as my landlord rather than a work colleague was not an issue as we always had a good friendship. All good things do however come to an end and the company decided that Billy's position as Training Manager was to be made redundant. This was one that I hadn't foreseen so as well as making myself redundant I was also making my friend and landlord redundant too!

***

Human resources can sometimes be a strange environment to work in with some brilliant but at times, strange people. All too often the HR department was very vocal in telling managers to front up and deal with their managerial issues. On one occasion I found myself working for a very affable HR Director who I'll call Ron Evans, on what happened to be the largest change management exercise that our company had faced.

The company had been purchased by a very large organisation for many millions of pounds and having acquired it, they realised that it was not profitable and that the business was not well positioned for the future. As a result major change was required or they would seriously consider their future involvement. Effectively the Board were told in no uncertain terms to produce a business plan which would bring profitability to the organisation.

In order to produce such a plan an elite group of specialists from throughout the business were locked away in a secret location and told to come up with the solution. When the plan had been produced and the cost of doing so evaluated we were to present the plan to the board of the parent company. Now this was a very major company with some very serious and bright individuals ready to pick our plan to pieces. Indeed, our plan entailed reducing the company from 3,000 to 1,100 staff and closing hundreds of branches. It also required a cash injection of twenty million pounds.

In light of the above the HR part of the plan was crucial and would clearly be placed under a microscope by the great and good on the board of the parent company. The months of work that had been put in to developing the plan was due to culminate in a presentation to the directors of the parent company which was likely to last several hours.

Obviously the preparation of this key presentation was stressful and involved working many long hours. My boss Ron Evans, was HR Director of our company and keen to ensure that he was well briefed before standing up in front of the parent company. I too was under pressure but somewhat relieved to think that at least Ron, as the senior person, would be delivering the HR piece. Indeed he had been privy to certain things that I had not been involved in for matters of confidentiality.

The day of the presentation arrived and I was up early ready to face the day. I was not expecting to go into the meeting but would be nearby in case Ron needed to discuss anything before or during the meeting. As I walked to the office at 8am I heard my mobile telephone ring and I could see that it was the HR team secretary Angela.

`Hi Ang,` I said, `how are you on this big day?`

`I`m OK,` she said, `but I`ve got some bad news for you.`

`OK,` I replied quite pensively, `what is that?`

Angela said, `Ron Evans has phoned in sick, and has asked that you do the presentation for him.`

After all of the HR preaching to Manager`s about facing up to their various issues it comes to probably the biggest day of my HR Director`s career and he has effectively bottled it and dropped me completely in the sh1t!

I was truly astonished by this dereliction of duty and never had the same time for him again. I duly took a number of deep breaths, pulled my trousers up tight and prepared for battle. Luckily for me I knew the plan quite well and managed to pull off the presentation to the best of my ability. There were a number of difficult questions to answer but I had anticipated them and had arguments ready.

Subsequently the parent company signed off to our proposals and agreed to the multi-million cash injection as well as the major changes to the business processes. Not long afterwards I arrived for work one day to be called up to the office of the Chief Executive. He read me a prepared statement saying that he had unfortunately had to place Ron Evans on `garden leave` and that he would not be returning to the company. It really was no great surprise in the scheme of things, obviously his "bottle job" had not gone unnoticed. I was now in charge of HR.

**

One of things that I always find slightly uncomfortable about working in HR is the fact that the HR community is often entrusted with developing the managers in a business, yet almost no one within the function has ever managed anything!

There are exceptions to any rule and I did have the privilege of working for one excellent HR Manager. Jim was a battle hardened Glaswegian in his mid forties who had learned his trade when dealing with trade unions in the bad old days of the 70`s and 80`s. He didn`t fit the usual profile of being a smooth, teflon coated HR figurehead. Instead he was practical and technically the most knowledgeable of any HR person that I worked for. Any line manager wanting sound advice would know that they would get that from Jim.

Blessed with a keen sense of humour, Jim also had the ability to pick up a guitar and have a sing song at the drop of a hat. That made him very popular amongst his staff. I gained an impression of his sense of fun in the first few weeks of working for him. We had been on a conference weekend and a group of about 15 of us had ended up in a hotel bedroom and were drinking long into the night. Unfortunately someone knocked red wine all over my new jumper. Quick as flash Jim legged it down to the –now closed- hotel bar, forced open the shutters and `borrowed` a bottle of white wine which he proceeded to empty over both me and my jumper. Job done although obviously in the morning there was a bit of explaining to do. A whip round

71

managed to straighten out the problem.

The organisational structure of that company had an area manager responsible for approximately 20 retail stores. Each retail store had a manager and perhaps 20 full and part-time staff. At the time a store would turn over about 2 million each per annum.

Amongst the other senior managers in the business, Jim occasionally had to deal with the area managers although he would normally deal with the more senior management. One or two of the area managers were old school and whose tendency was to totally disregard any form of guidance from HR, even when the guidance was given for sound legal reasons.

One particular Area Manager who Jim had to deal with was a total maverick and pig headed in the extreme. The area managers would be issued with recruitment documentation to ensure that the process was completed fairly and legally. I recall that this particular area manager had been reminded of the process on many occasions however for the "nth" time he had still managed to write to Jim on a scruffy piece of A4 paper with yet again no attempt to complete the job properly. Finally Jim lost patience, paid a visit to the gents toilet and returned with a piece of toilet roll on which he proceeded to describe the error of his ways to the area manager. He then popped it in the internal post. He never received incorrect documentation from that individual again.

Now at times Jim was abrasive and frequently rubbed the directors up the wrong way. Eventually in one of the frequent organisational changes the directors employed head hunters to bring in an HR Director above his head. I later found out that the cost of doing so amounted to over £50,000 given the size of new incumbent's salary with a national organisation.

We'll call the new HR Director 'William'. Now the new man was much younger than Jim and had a background in banking. Without wishing to put too fine a point on it, this individual was wet behind the ears, technically incompetent and quickly proved to be ineffectual. To those who were not HR professionals he could blag his way through with a combination of bluff, bluster and bullshit. To HR professionals it really was not difficult to see through him.

Now William probably realised that Jim could leave him standing technically and was a force with whom he could not deal. The obvious way out for our shallow new colleague was make Jim`s position redundant. As well as being wrong for the business, this was an incredibly unpopular with the HR team.

When William called a meeting to inform us of what he had done it was a particularly highly charged affair with one or two of my female colleagues becoming very emotional. His authority was not helped when he unveiled a single page of flipchart to try and convey his vision for the future. On the flipchart three out of the nine words were spelled incorrectly. How on earth could a team of professional HR people have confidence in someone who could not spell words such "yield" which he spelt "yeild", or "separate" which he spelt "seperate".

He managed to blag his way through for about 18 months and then left with a significant pay off. I would expect this to be a pattern for him for a number of years. Good work if you can get it !

***

William wasn`t the only `odd` HR Director with whom I worked. I recall another who liked to think that he was a fairly trendy flamboyant type and who certainly had a bit of an eye for the ladies. When he entered his mid-forties he suddenly decided to tint his hair red and grow a pony tail. This was at the time when we were trying to get the staff to look smart, professional and business like when dealing with customers!

He had the habit of saying `You`ll never work again` when faced with a colleague with whom he`d fallen out as if he was some sort of superior being who control all employment in the UK. On leaving the company one wonders if he ever worked again.

***

Working with some line managers was often a challenge as they sometimes viewed HR as a department with whom they should not engage unless they were absolutely desperate or totally out of their depth. Indeed at times you felt like you were viewed as somewhere between a "Shaman" and a "witchdoctor". One way of earning their trust was to prove that you were an expert in your field, perhaps in employment law for example. This was something which I made my field of expertise over the years and it proved to be essential in cementing relationships with operational managers.

There were many females employed in Human Resources and due to the fact that they were frequently dealing with some particularly difficult situations such as dismissals or redundancies, they had to be capable of being fairly tough if required. On one occasion I had just joined a company and as part of my induction was spending an hour with various departmental heads. I was sitting with the Recruitment Manager, Susan Jones, in her office which was located on a quiet floor amongst other senior managers and directors. She was going through an organisational chart and being extremely helpful and charming when her telephone rang.

`Excuse me,` she said, `this might be important and I`ll need to take it.`

`Of course` I replied, and sat back and relaxed for a moment.

Susan picked the phone up and said `Hello, Susan Jones Recruitment Manager, how can I help you.` I was struck by the lovely welcoming, smiley tone of her voice. The next thing I heard that took me a little by surprise was,
`FFFFFFFFFFUUUUUUUUUUUCCCCCCCCKKKKKKK OOOFFFFFFFFFFFFFF.` and the telephone was returned to its cradle with interest! You could have heard her expletive in the nearest town!

I heard doors up and down the corridor gently closing and for a brief moment I wondered whether anyone thought that the new employee may have upset her. One thing was for sure, I doubted that any of the senior managers within earshot would be trying to intimidate her any time soon.

`Everything OK I asked?`

`Yes, sorry,` she said, `some pervert just asked me what colours my knickers were!`

`I don`t think he`ll be doing that again in a hurry,` I said.

She laughed and replied `No, I don`t think so. Now where were we....`

***

Another female manager I worked for who I will refer to as Pat, was renowned for being tough and confrontational although, to be fair, she was a supportive character to those in her team if you were doing your job properly.

One of the area managers on my patch had never had any dealings with Pat as he worked many miles away from the Head Office. He managed around 20 stores and therefore he was running a business turning over about forty million pounds a year. Rather than reaching his position through the benefit of a privileged education he had risen up through the ranks in the school of `hard knocks` and occasionally his temper would boil over.   During management meetings he was known to rant and rave at some of his store managers perhaps in the way that you would expect a football manager to do. Lots of passion, numerous expletives!

Pat had occasion to speak to him one day and he made the mistake of trying to speak to her in similar tones to those which he spoke to managers when fired up.   Pat turned the air blue and called him the unprintable word [my mother will be reading this!] which all women hate which some refer to as `see you next Tuesday.` It was a classic case of a bully meeting a bigger and larger and more powerful bully and getting a proper caning. To his credit he never did complain, nor did he try to intimidate her again.

***

Whilst I am on the general subject of swearing [sorry again mother!] I want to get this story quickly out of the way. I`ve seen some strange behaviour in my time but this, from a senior manager, was some of the strangest.  I`ll call this individual Barry Cooper and he held quite a senior position in the company in management training.

Now Barry was quite a character with a great sense of humour and it

75

was good fun to be in his company. I'd heard on the grapevine that Barry had a rather unique way of answering the telephone and quite frankly I had dismissed the story as being just not probable and a bit of a "tall story". What I had heard was that he answered the phone in the most polite and perfect telephone rising tone with, `Fuck off Barry Cooper, how can I help you?` I would add that this was in the time before you could identify the caller with `Caller ID`.

I was fairly new to the company and I had cause to ring Barry about the forthcoming new Management Development Programme and to be fair, I was concentrating on the subject matter rather than thinking about his method of answering the telephone. He answered the phone with what *could* have been the phrase that I had heard about but the office was quite noisy and I couldn't be sure. Quite honestly it wasn't the right time and place to ask him about his telephone manner and we had a productive conversation about the new training programme and I soon forgot about it.

On my next visit to Head Office I thought that I would drop into Barry's office to have a more detailed chat about the Management Development Programme and its application to my part of the business. I tapped on his door and he readily invited me in. He could not have been more welcoming and was extremely professional in his knowledge of the subject matter. We had been chatting for about half and hour when the phone went. He said, `Sorry do you mind if I take this?`

`Not at all Barry,` I replied.

Without hesitation and in his perfect, almost tuneful telephone manner he said `Fuck off Barry Cooper, how can I help you?`

I nearly fell through the floor. I had never heard anything like this within a professional company before, or indeed, since. It could have been anyone from his boss to the Chief Executive, he had no way of knowing without Caller ID.

It was apparent that the caller did not respond to the `greeting` and they had a normal serious conversation about training issues for five minutes before the call ended.

`Just my little joke`, said Barry, `Now where were we...`.

Barry`s employment with the company lasted around 9-10 months and I never did find out why he left!

***

All HR professionals learned how to tell managers how to treat their employees in the correct way. Some HR managers however were completely incapable of replicating their advice when dealing with their own staff. The conveying of bad news about selection for redundancy should always be conveyed face-to-face. One HR manager who I worked for used to preach this gospel except of course, when he had to break that news to his HR staff. In those cases he seemed to prefer to convey the news over the telephone from a safe distance as he once did when making me redundant!

I recall another of my managers taking the easy way out. Kevin Welch had been invited to attend a regional meeting as an important and contentious item on the agenda was recruitment and the company was desperately trying to control costs and employees numbers. In order to do so a tedious recruitment process was put in place which I`ll call an Employment Authorisation Form [EAF]. This process was hugely time consuming paper based process and involved getting hold of all sorts of layers of management to sign it before it was approved.

The sheer length of time that it took was enough to deter most managers from even attempting to fill out one form unless they were totally desperate. In this particular region they were desperate but because it was located some distance from Head Office it would get overlooked. When they became aware that Kevin was going to make a royal visit to one of their monthly meetings they had expended much time and energy in producing approximately twenty four of these forms. They were delighted when Kevin promised to personally take them away and deal with them only to find that shortly after he left the meeting he lost all of the forms and they had to complete this annoying process all over again. Quite honestly they were livid and rightly so. Luckily for Kevin he had a cunning plan for the next meeting. Rather than go along and front up the anger he sent me instead.

His hair would have been curling at the way in which he was described in his absence. A pleasant fellow out of work, Kevin was a practiced `skiver` in work. How on earth he had achieved his position with such little knowledge, application and experience was a mystery to me. It was one of those annoying situations in life which most people will experience at one time or another when you find yourself reporting to someone who is far less capable but in far more senior position. At least I could consol myself in the knowledge that it was a contract which wouldn`t last forever.

***

Another work place situation which is not exclusive to HR is that which can occur when someone is promoted from a group of colleagues and then those who were previously friends of that person became direct reports under the new structure. This happened to me when I was one of four people who joined a company at the same time to fulfil identical brand new roles but in different parts of the country.

One of my colleagues who I`ll call Julie worked in the South-East. Unfortunately Julie had an obvious squint and whether this affected her ability to drive I don`t know although she was forever bumping her company car.

I`d heard one or two detrimental stories about Julie including that she was frequently late to important appointments with managers. If the appointment related to a disciplinary matter the manager was left sitting within the individual trying to make small talk whilst they waited for their HR colleague. What made things worse was a report that when she eventually turned up thirty minutes late she would be typically carrying bags of shopping.

Anyway after a while a promotion opportunity arose and I was fortunate enough to be selected. Julie was not happy about this as she was now reporting to me and as someone a little older, felt that she had have got the nod. We worked together for a while but she was clearly resentful.

Occasionally if she was visiting the Head Office we would be staying in the same hotel so we would politely meet up for an evening meal.

The hotel restaurant was quite large and occasionally it was hard to hear. During one such meal Julie looked quite serious, leaned forward slightly and spoke to me in a low voice, she said, `I don`t know whether you`ve noticed but I`ve had an operation on my thigh.`  Given the ambient noise I couldn`t be sure that I`d heard her correctly although she apparently had an obvious need to keep her voice down so I didn`t ask her to repeat herself.

I said `You wouldn`t notice, it doesn`t look like there is any difference at all.  Are you managing to get around OK?`

She replied `Yes, it doesn`t affect my getting around at all.`

`What about driving, can you drive OK, because I hear you`ve had a few bumps recently,` I said with a smile.

`Yes` she said, somewhat indignantly, if anything I can drive better now`.

`Good for you,` I said.

Her demeanour seemed to change and she seemed a little annoyed. She finished her main course and said brusquely `I`m going to turn in early I`ve a lot to do tomorrow,` and swiftly left for her room showing no signs of a limp.   I was a little confused by her behaviour and surprised that I hadn`t noticed her limping at all following her thigh operation. As the sweet course came and went and I sat there with my second pint of lager, it slowly dawned on me that she no longer had her squint!

***

As well as the HR staff I had the pleasure of working with some administrative colleagues. For a time I worked in a small regional office along with the Regional Operations Manager, his secretary Sandra and a young nineteen year old administrator by the name of Carly.

Sandra was a mature lady in her forties who had a great sense of humour. Her only hang up was regarding her weight. Every morning you would find an apple and a yogurt on her desk and that would comprise her lunch for the day. As I was trying to lose a few pounds as well we would often have a discussion about diets.

She said, ` I`m just not losing any weight it seems to get harder as you get older. All I have for lunch is a yogurt and an apple.`

`What about exercise?` I enquired.

She replied, `Well we do a bit of walking but it`s probably not enough.`

I said, `Do you snack between meals?`

She said, `......errr...I like a biscuit.`

I said, `but how many do you have a day?`

`About a packet,` she replied, `a packet of digestives.`

At that point Carly came over. She was a lovely girl and at the age of nineteen, no more than six or seven stones wringing wet.

I said, `Sandra, there`s no point in sitting there with an apple and a yogurt and then eating a complete packet of digestives each day, you`ll never lose your love handles like that!`

Sandra laughed hysterically but I noticed that Carly had gone a deep shade of red.

I said `Are you OK Carly?`

`Yes,` she said quietly.

`Carly do you know what "love handles" are?` said Sandra

Carly didn`t respond but looked embarrassed and went even more crimson than before.

`It`s the bits around your waist not your boobs!` laughed Sandra.

With that Carly laughed hysterically at her own embarrassment and scuttled off.

Carly`s naivety was an endearing quality and from time to time it would surface.  On one occasion she had helped me to place an advert which we expected to appear in the newspaper that day. I had popped out to the shops at lunchtime and bought a copy of the paper and also a copy of a local `What`s On` magazine entitled `Venue` to check out the entertainment for the weekend.

I had returned to my office and placed the folded newspaper, with the magazine inside it, on a table in my office. The magazine was completely obscured by the newspaper. Carly came in with some letters to sign and said, `has the advert gone in today?`

I said, ` I haven`t had time to have a look, why don`t you look in the paper it`s over there on the table.`

Carly picked up the newspaper and a copy of Venue magazine fell out on to the floor. She immediately coloured up and looked like a frightened rabbit.

I said, `Carly it`s not what you think, it`s an entertainment magazine.`

`Oh thank God.....,` she exclaimed, and let out a visible sigh of relief.

8 MANAGERS WITH PROBLEMS

I once worked for a company with many retail branches. Each retail branch was fairly large with a significant amount of annual turnover and staff. Many of the goods were high value and on occasions staff or indeed managers were known to steal them. In this line of business employees would move between ourselves and the competition and from time to time there would be takeovers and mergers which could lead to some strange situations where staff were re-acquainted with a previous boss who had moved company.

Equally employees who were well thought of in our organisation would move elsewhere and seek to return if it didn`t work out. On one occasion, Trevor, an area manager who managed about 15 stores, joined another company for promotion but his tenure only lasted about four or five weeks because he didn`t get on with his new boss. He subsequently asked to return to our business but as his former position as area manager was now filled, he was happy to return as a store manager on a lower salary.

He found himself working for an area manager who was formerly a peer but to whom he now had to answer. This particular area manager who I`ll call Roger, was particularly status driven and lacking in social skills. Whilst he was good with all aspects of merchandising stores and selling goods he was not well liked and was on something of an ego trip. He tended to often ignore company policy and to do things his own way. His manner at times when speaking to people was bordering upon pompous.

On his first meeting with Trevor on the latter's return to the business he said, 'so what's it like to be a store manager then Trevor?' with something of a smirk.

In fact the remark was not said with any trace of humour, only with a sense of pleasure and superiority at seeing his former colleague having to take a step backwards. He proceeded to give Trevor a fairly hard time over the following weeks and months which only hardened Trevor's resolve to do everything that he could to seek promotion at the next available opportunity.

With most retail businesses there seemed to be a reorganisation every quarter. With it often came redundancies for those who had fallen out of favour and opportunities for those who were in favour. As it happened the role of Area Manager reported to that of Regional Manager and the latter role was responsible for perhaps a hundred stores. Every so often the regions would change and the numbers of area and regional managers would also change. It was only a matter of 2-3 months before an opportunity arose and Trevor was restored to the position of area manager in a neighbouring location and was again a peer of Roger. Perhaps six months passed and a new regional manager position became vacant. Both Trevor and Roger applied and Trevor was successful. In the space of about one year Roger was now reporting to Trevor!

Whilst a reasonable man, Trevor never did forget the welcome that he had received from Roger on his return to the business and he proved to be a very hard task master for Roger in the months ahead. As the maverick that he was, Roger tried to continue to do things 'his way' and following one breach of policy too many, ended up being dismissed by Trevor.

Could Trevor have taken the decision to dismiss for a breach of policy had he chosen to do so? Yes. Was Trevor looking for an opportunity to get even? Probably. Did Roger give him that opportunity by behaving in a rude and superior manner? Definitely. It really does go to show that you should treat people with decency both on their way up through the business and on their down, otherwise it could come back to bite you on the backside.

***

There is no doubt that the business of management can be extremely stressful and different people cope with the pressures in different ways. For some it will be a visit to the gym after work. For others it will simply be spending time with the kids and completely forgetting about the job.

Others still, will find solace in the bottle. In my early days in an HR role I met with the manager of a manufacturing unit in Wales. Bill McIntosh was a Glaswegian who had grown up in the school of hard knocks. He was a skilled operator who knew all aspects of the business inside out. In any matter that you dealt with him you had to be on the case. In HR terms that meant that you had to know the law, particularly when he was dealing with disciplinary matters and the unions.

As Bill had many years experience he knew the law pretty well and was never going to have the wool pulled over his eyes by any HR manager who was `guessing` at it and was not professional. Luckily for me I had a very good grasp of employment law and therefore Bill would tend to deal with me as an equal. This was refreshing as he viewed previous HR Managers as little more than another `snout in the trough`, and therefore not someone who was actually contributing to the bottom line of the business and telling him something that he did not already know.

Bill was a hard man, he had to be. After all he was a Scotsman in a unionised manufacturing business in Wales. He was feared and respected in equal measure with a compassionate side as well as a tough side.

Now under the hard exterior he clearly needed something to get him through the day and I had it on very good authority from a source close to him that his method was have a bottle of whiskey in his desk draw and that he would start to drink from 8.30am. I have no doubt that this was true but it had gone on for so long that he was very skilled at hiding both the bottle and the effects of the booze. I certainly never heard his speech slurred or had complaints from staff about his drinking and if he was ever asked about it by a director he would tell them that if they could smell drink it would have been from the night before.

On occasions his boss the Production Director would have a look in his desk drawer to try and find the evidence but never could find it and turned somewhat of a blind eye because he was doing a great job and would have been impossible to replace. He got away with this because his factory was 90-100 miles away from Head Office and he therefore didn't get enough visits to catch him when he was drunk!

***

It was certainly not unheard of for employees to write in with anonymous letters to drop their manager in the brown stuff. Sometimes there was a specific reason for doing so, sometimes it was they just didn't like them. Staff from one south coast store wrote to me with what was basically a letter of mutiny. They wrote a letter signed by each and every member of staff stating that they could not bear to work for their manager for one day more!

It was the only time that I saw such a letter in my career and in some ways it resembled what you would find on a birthday card for a member of staff. It was one page, with a short statement surrounded by signatures, expressing their disapproval. Like the manager of a football club, once you've lost the dressing room the players will not perform as well for you and something needed to be done.

The Area manager was dispatched to investigate and ultimately found that at least some of the grievances were upheld. As a result the manager was deployed to another store and closely monitored.

***

On another occasion I received an anonymous letter which started off complaining that the manager of a particular unit was favouring one of the administrative staff. They also provided a reason for this which was that the member of staff spent a great deal of time in his office with her 'legs over her shoulders.'

Now I worked on a number of cases with this manager and had a good working relationship with him....albeit not the sort of working relationship alleged in the letter! When the allegation was put to him he immediately conceded that relationship had developed. As that member of staff worked for him it contravened the company policy precluding such relationships and they were informed that one of them would have to leave within an agreed time frame, which they subsequently did.

***

Sometimes it is the little things which bring a smile to your face and make the day go with a giggle. This story was told to me by a good friend of mine who I`ll name Richard Smith, who was responsible for a chain of 170 shops. These were relatively small shops which tended to employ about six or seven people and the majority by managed by females.

As a tall, smart, good looking and eligible fellow, his visits to his stores were often looked forward to by the female members of staff. If he had told me that himself I would have pulled his leg but it was in fact reported to me with a smile by his PA. In that case it must have been true.

Anyway, Richard was visiting a particular store one day which was located about two hours from his home. He was in the habit of arriving at a store at the opening time of 9am, often unannounced, to get sense of how a customer would find it. This would be the case even if it meant him waking at 6am and driving a couple of hours to get there.

On this particular day the traffic was bad and so during the trip he was constantly evaluating whether to stop at the motorway services and be late for opening or whether to press on and use the store facilities. In the end he preferred to make the statement that inspite of travelling a great distance, he had arrived at store opening time. Subsequently he arrived at the store at 9am in somewhat of a rush, absolutely desperate to use the toilet. Now his need on this occasion was greater than merely `number ones` and he was hoping beyond hope that the store would be open so that he could quickly access the facilities.

Fortunately he was in luck. The door to the premises was unlocked and he was able to head for the toilet in a relatively unhindered fashion. On reaching the toilet it was with a great sense of relief that he was able to sit down and enjoy the best part of the day. Having done so he reached out for the expect toilet roll. It was with a great sense of shock that he found that the toilet roll holder was empty.

He quickly looked around scanning the small room for a spare toilet roll. Unfortunately to his absolute dismay, there were no toilet rolls left. What was he to do? Here he was, the Regional Manager sitting on a toilet seat in one of his stores with his trousers around his ankles and without any toilet paper. It didn't help that as the toilet was positioned a long way from the store, there was little chance of any shout for assistance being heard.

Thinking quickly he patted his suit pockets hoping for any sign or a tissue or even.....errr....his handkerchief. No luck. There was nothing, absolutely nothing in this small office which he could use as an emergency substitute toilet roll.

He sat there for seemed like an age, doomed to his fate but desperately seeking solutions. In his career he had completed numerous managerial training courses telling him how to deal with dismissals, profit and loss, leadership, health and safety etc but right at this moment, none were of any use whatsoever.

A full fifteen minutes of sheer terror had gone by the time that he heard the sweet words 'Mr Smith, I've left some toilet roll outside the door for you.' Happy days, it was the voice of the female manager who had popped out to the local supermarket for some supplies. All of a sudden those irrational thoughts of ripping up his shirt had disappeared......!

***

On occasions people who should know better act with incredible stupidity and lack of judgement. The following story is a case in point.

Two employees, a field sales manager and his line manager, decided to telephone a female employee who had been excessively absent from work. They suspected that she was not so much sick being a bit of a malingerer. In order that they could both hear the call they placed the phone on loudspeaker. Unfortunately their colleagues' phone went to voicemail and the pair of managers hung up without leaving a message. They then had a conversation between themselves along the lines of how it was "such a pity that she was so lazy and always on the sick as or the rare occasions when she turned in, she had a great arse and tits."

Unfortunately, they had failed to replace the receiver correctly and the whole conversation was recorded on the females voicemail! They were later both dismissed and the female enjoyed a continued bout of paid sick leave for a very long time!

***

Whilst we are on the subject of managerial stupidity I recall another incidence which is really best confined to the history books. Anyone who has ever undertaken interviewing knows that if you see a significant number of people during one day it can be difficult to put a face to a name. These days everyone has a mobile phone so it is not difficult to take a quick photo to aide your memory. Back in the day it was really down to the quality of your note taking.

Psychological experiments had proved that it was much easier for an interviewer to remember candidates at the start or the end of the day. Those in the middle were a little more difficult to recall. One of our managers decided to develop his own unique way of recalling all interviewees. He would draw a very quick sketch of one of their memorable features on their application form.

This approach worked for him for some months and indeed years. He might quickly draw a red jumper on the application form or for example the colour of a tie. It could be an item of clothing or a physical characteristic such as an indication of height. It all acted to aid his memory and therefore, in his mind, gave everyone a fair and equal chance at interview.

Unfortunately for him his technique did become unstuck. One memorable candidate was a young lady of impressive figure. In the heat of the moment all that he could think of was to draw an impressive bosom on her application form. Had there not been an issue with the recruitment of this staff member the application form could have been locked away in the corner of his office never to see the light of day. In actual fact someone felt that they had been treated unfairly by not being selected during interview and all applications forms were produced to review the fairness of the appointment. His little sketches then came under a great deal of scrutiny and the image of the bosom resulted in a disciplinary hearing.

***

In one company I worked for we had a problem with staff theft due to the high value of some of goods sold. It was a fairly common occurrence for staff members to be occasionally tempted and be caught stealing stock. From time to time managers would also be caught and would face disciplinary action ultimately resulting in dismissal.

The company had recently taken over a smaller competitor and we were getting to know the newly acquired employees. In one store the manager was a middle aged man who I'll call Henry Smith. Now Henry was about 6' 4' tall and powerfully built with an air of authority. He had apparently worked at a more senior level in his previous company although now had returned to his current status.

The local Area Manager Peter Gunter, managed about 15 stores. He too, had come from the acquired company but when that company was acquired he was retained as an area manager and kept some of his former store and was given some new stores from the existing company. He was well known in the industry and had a reputation of somewhat of a bully. That said, he did produce results at least in terms of sales figures.

For some reason I'd also heard that Peter Gunter was a member of a fairly secretive 'lodge', perhaps similar in some ways to a Masonic lodge. Now I don't have any problem with Masonic lodges in particular, after all my grandfather served in both World Wars and was very happy to be a member of a masonic lodge. He was a working man, the sort who stood up when the national anthem was played during the Queen's speech on Christmas Day. I was however aware that they have some strange rituals and some of them are very hung up with rank with the chief being held in great esteem and carrying a lot of authority and power.

The company audit and security team had been looking at Henry Smith`s store and found a number of major issues with everything from stock loss to Henry selling items in the store which were not owned by the company. In other words he was selling some goods that he had sourced himself! Indeed the security team had bought some in the interests of evidence gathering.

This was quite a bizarre situation and presumably he had been doing this for some time but in the previous smaller company he was too clever to be caught. He was rumoured to throw money around as if it was going out of fashion when in reality his salary was unlikely to sustain such spending unless he had another revenue stream. With the takeover of his company Henry was now exposed and there little he could do about it.

Henry was interviewed and duly suspended pending his disciplinary hearing. I was dispatched with his manager Peter Gunter, to conduct the hearing which took place in another store in the city. Despite his reputation as a bully, Gunter was quite a small man in his mid-fifties. He must have conducted hundreds of disciplinary hearings over the years but this was the first that I had attended with him.

Never before had I seen someone of his experience and years shake so much before and during the hearing. This was someone who was clearly terrified. When Henry Smith entered the meeting room he towered over Gunter with an air of menace. This was not someone who had come prepared with a few excuses, this was someone who knew his fate but who wanted to intimidate Gunter and make him squirm. For most of the meeting he sat and stared at Gunter barely blinking and occasionally making a very short response to a question.

Luckily for Gunter the case was watertight as on the key points the security and audit departments had presented him with evidence that could not be challenged. He had sold his own goods through the store, there was massive stock loss, he had misappropriated items, the list went on and on. The disciplinary hearing briefly adjourned to allow Gunter to think about his decision. Gunter was in such a state that I wondered whether he would be able to speak when we re-started the meeting.

It was unusual to see someone like Gunter, who was a bully by nature, shake so much when conveying the bad news to Smith. He was visibly shaking and with a noticeable tremor in his voice. Luckily when we reconvened, Gunter was able to get the words out and told Smith that he was being dismissed for gross misconduct and that his company vehicle was being seized with immediate effect. Smith sat in his seat for what seemed like several minutes with his gaze intently fixed on Gunter as the latter shrivelled in his seat. Eventually Smith rose to his feet still staring, and very slowly left the room leaving Gunter in psychological tatters.

I felt that Gunter`s response to dealing with this issue was disproportionate and surprisingly weak. After all, he had been in the industry for twenty years and must have dealt with numerous cases like this. I couldn`t quite work out why he behaved as he did until someone whispered in my ear that Gunter was a member of the same secretive lodge that Smith was a member of but that Smith was the most senior person in that lodge. Oh dear, Gunter had just sacked the "Chief Moose" in his lodge!

***

Obviously some strange things happened in this particular city. In one of the other stores the female assistant manager was living with someone of dubious integrity. She was one of two people who had access to the store and the alarm system. One night the store had been burgled and extensively cleared out. This was a proper professional job where they would have spent a couple of hours in the building. When the Police caught the culprits it turned out to be the partner of the assistant manager. After a thorough investigation the police were satisfied that she was not involved and that he had the store keys copied.

In another part of the city one of the items that were sold were washing machines. In one store they had actually plumbed in one of the washing machines that was supposed to be on display and were using it to do their washing!

***

At one point in time I was briefly responsible for covering 12 stores in Northern Ireland. This was before the Good Friday agreement and during this time the troubles were still in full swing. It was well known that the petty cash was regularly used to pay off the local para-militaries and from time to time there would be an armed robbery at a store.

One week there was a robbery at a store in a Catholic area. This meant that the manager was required to go to the local police station to make a statement which was an extremely difficult and stressful thing for him to do as he was worried that he may be perceived as a grass or `tout` which could mean punishment of death. Nevertheless he bravely made the trip.

The following week he caught his assistant manager stealing cash from the company. He was essentially trying to fund his lavish wedding and had turned to crime to do so.

Under normal circumstances the company would always prosecute which meant that the manager would once again be asked to go and make a statement to police which would have been the second time in a week. He was so stressed by this that he ended up on prescription medication and the company took an exceptional route by just dealing with the matter internally without involving the Police to protect the health of the manager.

***

It is not uncommon for the owner of a company to cause serious problems for the manager. I recall working for a large organisation and hearing a story about the owner which would have occurred in the 1970`s. The company employed thousands of staff many of whom worked in the transport of goods at depots throughout the country.

The owner was ex-services and had some very forthright views on certain aspects of appearance and background. He absolutely *hated* overweight people or men with beards. He would often visit his depots and so if it was known that he was visiting anyone who was overweight or bearded would have to be sent out in the van and not venture back to depot until after he had left.

He also had another peculiar habit which was to instantly promote a member of staff who was ex-services at the expense of someone who was not. For example he attended a management meeting with a number of managers and supervisors. When he discovered that one of the supervisors was ex-services he instantly promoted them and demoted a manager, on the spot, in front of everyone at the meeting! That sort of behaviour is unthinkable now but in the 1970`s the world was a different place, particularly to a maverick owner.

9 IN WORK, OUT OF WORK

In HR you frequently find yourself dealing with all manner of issues at work and very many of these have the capability of crossing over and affecting someone`s private life. Some issues are very serious indeed and can involve anything from an individual passing away during their employment with the company, to a serious criminal matter. Some other issues seem less important but involve a major point of principle, and something over which people are not prepared to make any concessions.

One company that I worked for decided to bring in Sunday working on a rota basis, an issue which went down very badly with staff and unions alike. It was one of those things that had been very poorly thought through by senior management. There seemed to have been no consideration as to why we actually wanted to bring it in. For example was there really a demand from customers to have visits from engineers on a Sunday? I found no evidence that there was, although HR was tasked with the responsibility of forcing it through. This entailed a major consultation with affected staff and a great deal of worry about important issues such as family life etc on the one day that families could actually guarantee to spend together.

It many of these situations a financial carrot is dangled to persuade those involved that it would be a good idea. They then have a certain amount of time to sign up to the idea. One of my engineers however was an extremely pedantic and fairly odd individual who was absolutely determined that he was not going to work on a Sunday.

Now I actually respect this sort of stance because personally I too, would be loathed to do so. His reason for not doing so was that he was a model boat enthusiast and that he liked to sail his model boat on a Sunday.

In view of his refusal to accept the change to his contract we had arranged a consultation on 11th September 2001, which became known as 9/11. In this business there were TV`s in every office and minutes before the meeting planes had hit the World Trade Center and the appalling loss of life had begun. Anyone who watched the attack was shocked to the core.

The attack put many issues in life into perspective however Immediately following the attack I had to sit through 2 hours with this individual telling me in a particularly rude and pedantic manner how he was not prepared to work one Sunday in every six because he wanted to sail his model boat. In the scheme of things it actually felt that he was lucky to be able to see another Sunday, whatever he chose to do with it.

After a very painful two hours with him we adjourned and eventually he was offered a redundancy package which he decided to take because he was able to combine it with a job offer and therefore pocket a very handsome pay off. At all times he was rude and obnoxious however reasonably I, or my colleagues, tried to deal with him.

He effectively left the company leaving a very bad taste in the mouth of his line manager and anyone in HR who had the bad luck to have any time with him. At the time we wondered how he would get on with the new company because he was very `old school` in the sense that he was not flexible and had pretty much `done his own thing` in the workplace for many years. That is all very well when you have a degree of seniority and length of service with a business but if you go to work elsewhere it is almost never appreciated.

Life does however have a way of getting even and a matter of 6-8 weeks after he left the company he telephoned me with an unusually polite tone in his voice to say that things hadn`t worked out where he was in the new company. Apparently he had suffered illness and they had quickly terminated his employment. The chances are that they actually saw an opportunity and had taken it.

He asked whether there was there any chance that he could have his old job back and added that he would be happy to work Sundays as required. Sometimes things occur which go beyond the point of return and of course the answer was negative. The irony of ironies was that the Sunday working idea didn`t have legs and was ceased some weeks later.

***

It never ceases to amaze me how out of work activities can impact on someone working life. Frequently a company will employ family relations in their business and most of the time there are no problems. Normally a line reporting relationship is not allowed so for example, a husband could not directly report to his wife or vice versa. If a relationship was to develop, as they often do, most organisations require that one of the people moves to another department so a secretary may have to move departments to work for another manager. In small business units it is not uncommon for one person involved to actually leave the company.

Imagine the complications if a manager was conducting an appraisal for their partner and there was a work performance issue. It can also get complicated when it comes to awarding pay rises. I recall a female manager giving her female assistant manager a pay rise which was more than double the annual pay review. This was a serious breach of a particularly strict company policy and after an investigation it transpired that they were conducting an affair. The results of the investigation were that there was no other reason for the increase than the fact that they were in a relationship. The manager was subsequently dismissed.

On another occasion in a different company, there was a husband who worked as a production supervisor and his wife who worked as a payroll clerk in the accounts department. They were both well regarded as employees and never came into contact except at lunch times as their respective work places were in separate parts of the building.

The wife was a quiet and fairly prim and proper individual who was well educated and smartly dressed. She was the sort of person who could be relied upon to complete her work accurately and on time, a matter of great importance to the payroll department. The husband was much more `rough and ready` although competent as a supervisor and well liked.

Normally the factory was productive and any stoppage to the production line was frowned upon and the management would act quickly to get things moving. One day the factory manager noticed that work had stopped and a crowd had gathered around an employee's machine. He was known as `Bob` and was a particularly slimy and at times, smelly individual. He was the sort of man with whom you would make excuses not to shake his hand!

On getting closer he could see that the group were looking at, and laughing at, a pornographic magazine. The particular feature that they were looking at was known as `Readers Wives` and spread across the feature, in poses that would give credit to a Russian gymnast, was the payroll clerk. Her husband had only gone and sent racy photos of his wife to a magazine which apparently was subscribed to by a work colleague!

I must admit that I expected the couple to immediately resign and leave the company in shame. Not a bit of it! They carried on as usual without even breaking stride, although it must be said that no-one really looked at her in the same light ever again.

***

Work for senior managers inevitably means the occasional social outing with the partners of work colleagues. I recall a previous manager by the name of `Nigel Wicks` telling me about an incident that happened to him and his wife Marie at one such event attended by our company.

The couple had been invited to a `black-tie` do at a posh London hotel at the behest of Nigel's line manager who was Rex Clifford, a Board Director of this well known company. The event had been organised by a supplier and involved some top quality entertainment as well as the usual opportunity to make business contacts. Clifford's wife Becky was also in attendance although neither Nigel or Marie had ever met Becky on a previous occasion.

As the Director and his wife only lived a few miles away it was decided that they would order a taxi and pick up Nigel and his wife Marie on the way.   It was further planned that they would share a taxi home at the end of the evening.   On the way to the hotel everything went smoothly. Becky was personable and very smartly dressed, as you would expect from someone who was `well heeled`.

The evening too was enjoyable and it is fair to say that all had enjoyed a drink.   In fact Becky, the Director`s wife, had probably enjoyed a few drinks than the others put together. At the end of the evening each partner was presented with a gift bag by the hosts. In keeping with the profile of the guests and the venue, the gift bag contained some expensive items of perfumery and other items worth a few hundred pounds in total.   Marie was very pleased with her gift bag as the perfume was a particular favourite of hers.

Just prior to leaving Marie paid a visit to the ladies toilets leaving her gift bag on the table in the space where she had been sitting. On her return it has disappeared. She asked Becky if she had seen anyone remove it but Becky said that she hadn`t. Not wishing to cause a fuss she decided not to progress the matter even though she was disappointed that someone had taken her gifts.

A London cab arrived to take both couples back to their respective homes. During the course of the journey Nigel found himself sitting next to Marie. At one point she had the need to retrieve the house keys from her bag and to do she hauled the bag onto her knee and opened it next to Nigel. In the course of rummaging around Becky she displaced a few items, two of which were the gift bags with which both women had been presented. Nigel was a little shocked by this but again decided not to cause a fuss as it was his boss`s wife.

Shortly after the taxi arrived at their house and in the course of saying goodbye to Clifford and Becky, Nigel leaned over to give Becky a peck on the cheek.   In the process of doing so she moved her position, gave him a smacker on the lips and promptly inserted her tongue into his mouth! Neither Clifford nor Marie had seen the incident as they were politely saying goodnight to each other.

Well, ask yourself a question, what would you do? At the end of a pleasant evening your boss's wife has stolen a gift worth a few hundred pounds and then kissed you full on the lips when no more than a yard from her husband. In his typically English way Nigel decided not to mention either event and to let 'sleeping dogs' lie.......

***

It was a regular occurrence for staff to be put up in hotels when working a long way from home on matters such as new store openings. These events were huge drains on time and resources and inevitably called for quite a number of people staying away.

With all of the hard work undertaken during the day it was likely there would a degree of 'letting off steam' in the evenings although most people would go to the gym, go for a swim or relax with a couple of beers. There are however always a few who take things too far. On one occasion a group of perhaps twenty employees were staying in a well known hotel chain not far from Heathrow.

A few of them had been up drinking and at 3am one morning, one of them thought that it would be great fun to take a fire extinguisher off the wall and let it off in the room of his colleague. Being no expert in the world of fire extinguishers, he expected his pal to get a few squirts and perhaps slightly soaked from an expected jet of water. What actually happened was that he had picked the extinguisher which is filled with powder and which does not stop once you let it off.

The result of this escapade was that the extinguisher set off the fire alarm and caused the complete hotel of 250 people to be evacuated into the car park. In addition the powder caused thousands of pounds worth of damage to the room resulting in a disciplinary for the embarrassed and quickly sobered staff member!

***

It is only natural for work colleagues to enjoy a drink from time to time and that to an out of work incident related to one of our Welsh stores. The manager had employed a newish sales executive and he had been working at the store for around 6 months without incident.

One evening after work a few members of staff decided to go to a local pub. After a couple drinks the manager, who was something of a joker and knew various magic tricks, said, ` I`ll show you a magic trick, if you can guess how I do it I`ll give you £10. If you can`t guess how I do it you, you give me £10. Are you up for the challenge?`

`Yes I`ll have some of that,` said the new salesman.

The manager produced a pack of cards and showed him a trick. The salesman had no clue how it was done and handed over a hard earned £10 note. He then said, `Ok, give me a chance to win my money back. Show me the trick again for double or quits.`

`Ok,` said the manager, `its £20 to me if you can`t get it, or £20 to you if you can?`

`That`s it,` replied the salesman.

The manager shuffled the cards and again showed him the trick and the salesman had no idea how it had been done.

`Right hand over the £20 said the manager laughing`

Before he could blink the salesman had punched him and knocked him out!

I was left to deal with the remnants of a situation whereby a manager had been assaulted by a member of staff and knocked unconscious outside of the workplace! In the cold light of day it didn`t take too much to consider that if he was capable of assaulting his manager, this individual could easily assault a difficult customer and we therefore terminated his employment.

***

The behaviour and misjudgement of some people in their lives outside of work will never cease to amaze me. On one occasion a couple of engineers were disgruntled over changes that the company was making to working practices. This was in spite of the fact that the company was going through a process of consultation and offering financial incentives for people to sign up for the new terms and conditions.

Instead of registering their concern and discussing the matter as adults, they set up what they thought was an anonymous website with the intention of deriding the company. The website was something of a spoof with photo's of company vans and thinly disguised logo's of a very similar look!

Did they serious think that they could get away with this without getting caught? A quick check with internet registrars gave the name of the culprits who were incredibly embarrassed and shamefaced when confronted with the evidence and immediately removed the site from the web to head off any disciplinary action.

***

Another memorable example of when the personal life of an employee impinged upon their working life occurred just before Christmas one year. At this particular company all post was opened by the receptionist and distributed to the appropriate department via a `pigeon hole`.

On this cold December day a package arrived for a member of staff addressed to the company but marked `private and confidential` and `for the attention` of the person, who'll I'll call Richard West. As there had been a significant reorganisation ongoing, the receptionist was under the impression that the department had been closed and individual had been made redundant. She therefore decided to open the package to try to decide where she should forward it to.

I should comment here that Reception at this company was open to both the public and customers and frequently visitors would be congregated around the reception desk.

As the receptionist opened the package a total of six videos fell out onto her desk. They were plain in terms of packaging with just a handwritten label on each. There was no letter with the package or any information from the sender. Trying to get a clue as to what this was about, the receptionist read the video cassette labels.

My office was located by the reception area and following a knock on door the receptionist entered looking a little flustered and red in the cheeks, `You better have a look at these,` she said, and handed me the package. I think Richard West has been made redundant and I don`t know where to send them`.

Now being an HR manager who liked to be accessible to the staff, my office door was always physically open. Anyone walking past the office could look in and speak to me if necessary. I also had a TV and video player in my office as I often used it for training sessions and induction purposes. I selected a sample video, walked over to the TV, switched it on and inserted the cassette.

`Wait there a second,` I said to the receptionist, and I returned to my desk, turned up the volume on the remote and waited for the film to start. No sooner had I sat down could the sounds of passion be heard booming out from the video. Any senior manager walking past my office at 9.30am on that December day in that split second would have seen the HR Manager with the receptionist apparently watching a porno film in work time!

I quickly extricated myself from the seat and ran to the video to turn it off! The fact that the video contained exclusively males was not lost on either myself or the receptionist. Would that have made it even worse for any passing colleagues? I`ll never know.

The receptionist said `If you give me his address I`ll send it on to him`.

I replied, `there`s no need for that, his department hasn`t moved yet, he`s still working here in the building.`

I must confess that I was a little surprised that Richard West, a married man in his early sixties, had apparently had this particular video content sent to his place of work. I said to the receptionist, `Can you give him a ring and tell him come down and collect his parcel and I`ll then have a chat.`

`Ok,` she replied, `I`ll let you know when he turns up.`

She returned to reception but telephoned me almost immediately to say that whilst she was in my office, he had emailed to enquire as to whether a parcel had arrived for him. I asked her to email back and inform him that it was ready for collection now.

Within a couple of minutes Richard West had arrived at reception and the receptionist gave me a call. I walked out to the reception area and the colour drained from his face almost immediately. I said, `Richard can I have a chat a second in my office?`

Now in terms of any potential disciplinary offences the only one possible allegation was that he had brought the company into disrepute by having pornographic materials delivered to his workplace to an area which was frequented by customers. His likely defence would be that he did not expect his parcel to be opened.

I sat him down and said `Do you know why I want to have a chat with you?`

He said, `Is it because I`ve had a parcel delivered to work.....it`s ...errrr...a Christmas pressie for the wife.`

For a moment my mind boggled as I had the vision of the package being produced from underneath the tree on Christmas morning and presented to his wife. Would she really be that happy receiving half a dozen gay porn videos from her husband?!

` I said, it is a little more that, any other ideas?`

`Is it because of the indecent material?` he volunteered.

`Yes,` I said.

Once again his face sank and I gently explained to him that his sexuality was not of concern to either company or myself but that it was not acceptable to have such materials sent to his place of work and to any area whereby they could be seen by the public.

`I`ll never do it again,` he said, and `Oh, can I take them with me now?`

`I think that you better had,` I replied

***

Many people are keen to leave behind the corporate drudgery and start their own business. Wanting to leave and actually doing it are two quite different things. In reality it is very difficult to fund the start up of a business and the period of time when the business is not making any money. First you could have stock to buy, premises to rent, or office equipment to acquire. Then there are costs for advertising, staff, vehicles etc. For some people it takes a windfall such as being left money in a will. For others a redundancy payment and the loss of a job could provide sufficient momentum. There is also another group of people who decide to start their business whilst still being employed by the company.

For most people it is however, not that easy to start a business and I have known of employees typing up Indian restaurant menus at work and taking orders for takeaway meals on their company mobile phone. At another company managers were provided with company cars and free fuel. This was massively profitable for the driver when it was used as a taxi on the weekend!

One employee was trying to start a business repairing computers and whilst he would visit the customer on business he would try to the conversation round to computers and any repairs necessary. He would then return later and normally used `bootleg` software to effect a dodgy repair and which ultimately led to his dismissal.

10 POLICE MATTERS NASTIES AND NUTTERS

With the sort of issues that an HR manager deals with you often find that employment related matters are inextricably linked to the criminal law. An obvious and constantly recurring theme is where an employee steals items from their workplace. When that happens one of the most important questions is whether to involve the police or not.

One disturbing case that I worked on involved the issue of child pornography in the work place. In the company that I worked for there was a small section of 3-4 employees who would work out of office hours. Often they would cover until midnight and for the purposes of their work they needed access to the internet. I'll use the name Serge Kaley to identify the employee in question.

Nearly all of the security team were former detectives who either retired from the police or decided to make a career in security as civilians. I always worked closely with them and on this occasion I received a telephone call from them asking if they could come straight down to my office to discuss a sensitive case. Obviously I agreed and within seconds they had appeared at my door.

Security explained that they had received a call from an employee alleging that they had seen a colleague, Serge Kaley, viewing child pornography. Apparently this had occurred at around 10pm at night as they had been walking past his desk. He had tried to shut the pages down but hadn't been quick enough to do so without them noticing. They had decided to behave as if they hadn't seen the image and then to report the matter rather than to raise it with him directly.

The security department had then conducted investigations and could see that over a period of weeks he had been using his work computer to enter chat rooms frequented by children using the name `Perv Daddy`. He had also been viewing pornographic material of children from the ages of around 6 months to early teenage years. Even though he had been married for around a year, he was looking primarily at images of young boys. It was truly shocking and one of the most disturbing cases that I ever had to deal with.

Clearly this was a case which was likely to include both employment and criminal issues and we were determined to deal professionally with the matter to ensure that we dealt with employment law and company policy efficiently but without prejudicing the a potential police case.

In fact it was extremely important to us that we looked at the wider picture in this case. We felt that from a community point of view this individual needed to face the full weight of the criminal law. What can happen in some other cases is that the company will first act to protect commercial interests rather than to be concerned with the criminal law. This was not going to happen here.

Security had done their homework on this one and produced all of the documentary evidence which was needed for us to put to Serge Kaley at the investigation interview. These included print outs of his visits to chat rooms and a sample of images which he had been viewing. This individual was not someone that I had met before although I was aware that he had a reputation for being cocky and rude from his dealings with a colleague over a separate unrelated issue. We decided to interview him at the very earliest time so that we could promptly deal with the case.

When he arrived for work for his shift he was informed by his supervisor to report to HR. Waiting for him was one of the most professional security managers on the team and myself. He walked into my office with an air of arrogance.

`Do you know why we want to talk to you?` I said.

`No.` he replied flippantly.

The security manager then proceeded to show him the documentary evidence including times and dates of visits to chatrooms, transcripts of conversations that he had been involved with and some of the photographic images. In over twenty years in HR never had I seen someone disintegrate in front of me like Serge Kaley. Within seconds he was a jibbering wreck as his perverted world fell all about him. His denials were unintelligible between his sobs and he must have realised that his seedy activities were about to be exposed. In seconds he was facing the loss of his job, the prospect of prison as a sex offender, and all of his family and friends knowing about his dirty little secret.

As we were getting little sense out of him from an investigatory point of view, we felt that the `greater good` would be served by immediate police involvement. We were very keen not to give him the chance to destroy evidence and we were also unclear whether he had access to children. We did not however tell him about our planned police involvement, we told him to sit in an adjoining office whilst we would consider what action to take. After he did so we called the police and they agreed to come to the office.

After about five minutes I decided to check on him in the office. When I opened the door I could see blood of his wrists where he had used a broken ID card to try to cut himself. To be honest the cuts were not so deep that they would have caused serious injury and we asked the first aider to patch him up prior to the police arrival. When I informed security what had happened they said, `you should have given the bastard another couple of minutes to do a proper job!`

It wasn`t long before a couple of policemen arrived at reception. He was duly arrested and suffered the embarrassment of being escorted from the building in handcuffs. It must have come as a great shock to his wife when she arrived home from her work at a bank to find the police searching her home. Indeed you can only have sympathy for someone in the position. The police seized his computer and with it found numerous incriminating images of children. It will have probably come as a greater shock to his wife when she realised that he appeared to be interested in young boys. That said, by the time that he went to Court and pleaded guilty to the offences, she was visibly pregnant in the public gallery. Presumably she must have either forgiven him or just buried her head in the sand.

***

Under the nasties section in this chapter comes an extremely distasteful case that I dealt with some years ago. Essentially this involved a matter of long term sickness. One of the employees in a warehouse had taken frequent periods of sick absence during his employment. His manager had been very inefficient in dealing with him and he had been allowed to get away with taking time off with virtual impunity. There was very little suggestion that he was suffering from a genuine illness and of course his absence put continuous and sustained pressure on his more reliable colleagues.

When I inherited his unit I was made aware of him and decided to take an interest in managing his health and attendance. Just before Christmas one year he again phoned in sick and provided a self certification form which would last for a total of seven days. He was able to do this without a visit to the doctor for seven days before needing to get a doctor`s certificate for the eighth day. Seven days came and went and his manager had not heard from him. I told his manager to get in touch with him to tell him to bring in his doctor`s certificate.

When the manager contacted him he informed his manager that he was very sorry but his 14 year old brother had been killed in a road accident in Surrey on Christmas Eve and that as a result his mother had a breakdown and had been committed to a mental health unit. He said that he was trying to resolve the issues arising from this tragedy and needed time. Of course the manager was sympathetic and told him to take the time that he needed but to keep in touch.

After a week or so we had heard nothing from him and given his previous unreliability I decided to research the details of the accident. Firstly I had to establish whether there was actually a record of a road traffic accident in Surrey on Christmas Eve resulting in the death of a 14 year old boy. I checked a number of sources from the internet to the register of births marriages and deaths, to the local police. Of course there had been no such accident, his brother was alive and well.

I further checked his personnel records to find that this wasn`t the first time that he had taken significant amounts of time off for an alleged death in his family. He had taken about six weeks off about two years previously relating to the death of his Aunty Winnie from Jamaica who had apparently raised him from a child. He had claimed that Aunty Winnie was like a mother to him and the company had been very supportive at that time and had paid full salary so that he could return to Jamaica for the funeral etc.

He was called in for an investigation interview and when asked to confirm the name of the relative who died during his six week absence two years before, he couldn`t even recall the name of the relative who had `died`. When asked about the death of his 14 year brother he suddenly became very vague about times, dates and the location of the accident. Furthermore he didn`t even know where his mother was in hospital.

This did really leave a bad taste in my mouth. I had heard of every possible reason for sickness absence in my time but to state that your young brother had died was really the lowest of the low.

After a thorough investigation there was plenty of evidence to suggest that he had falsified documentation and obtained company sick pay by deception and he was duly dismissed for gross misconduct.

***

In a large company it was always possible that you employed someone with previous criminal convictions from time to time. Under the Rehabilitation of Offenders Act it was quite legal for a person to say that they had no convictions if a period of time had passed since the conviction. This law gave them the chance to change their ways and rehabilitate into society.

Of course there were times when the company would receive an anonymous call regarding an employee effectively with the mischievous intention of `dropping them in it!` Motives for so doing were numerous although I would suggest that top of the list was an ex-partner following a breakup of the relationship.

One call I received related to someone who was employed by the company and had been working for us for 4-5 years in a role which involved cash handling. The call suggested that in the past she had worked for a competitor but had been dismissed for a large scale theft. The store that she worked at for all of that time had an excellent record for accounting and no record of stock or cash loss. We checked her application form and she had not disclosed any criminal convictions even though she should have done in this case.

It was one of those cases where the instinct was to dismiss her however we referred the matter to the company lawyers and they said to dismiss would be likely to be found to be unfair at Employment Tribunal so in view of the fact that store accounts and admin were in perfect order we took the view to retain her services and take no action.

****

In one company I worked for I received a promotion and ended up with four direct reports and around 45 employees. One of my direct reports was obviously a bit peeved at not getting the job. She liked to try to show me that she was still in control [at least in her mind!] and so she was in the habit of telling me something when it had already happened. In this way she was just "letting me know" rather than asking me if a particular decision was OK in advance of the event. Now ninety per cent of the time this approach was OK and to be honest I didn`t want trivia brought to me every two minutes. Part of the skill for her managing upwards however, was to anticipate what I might consider to be important and then refer it to me. Unfortunately she wasn`t very capable of this skill and that was coupled with bouts of what I can only refer to as `dopiness`.

One day she popped her head round my door and said, `just to let you know, the post room clerk I have just recruited has a previous conviction, OK?`

These were times of economic hardship and there were not many jobs around. She was trying to make a speedy retreat when I said

`What was the previous conviction for?`

`Kidnapping,` she replied.

`KIDNAPPING, ARE YOU SERIOUS`?   I bellowed. `Do you know what a serious offence kidnapping actually is?  What were the circumstances of the kidnapping?`

`I`m not sure, I`ll ask him.`

`So you didn`t even ask why he was convicted of kidnapping?` I said with some intent in my voice.`

`Er...no,` she said.

`How long was his sentence?`

`I`m not sure..,` she sheepishly replied.

It took my breath away. What did she seriously think that he done, stolen a chicken from the local farm? We had a duty of care towards out staff, what about that?

When she did actually ask him to describe what had happened it involved him bundling someone into the boot of a car and driving off for a hundred miles before assaulting them. It related to a fairly recent matter from which they had not long been released. Whilst I am all for rehabilitation of offenders, I also had a duty of care to the other staff and customers at a time when the supply of labour was plentiful. He was not retained.

***

It will never cease to amaze me how a reckless decision can result in a course of action which can turn a minor problem into something much more serious. One case in point involved the stupidity of an engineer.

In the course of their work they used a powerful and expensive drill. This was an important tool and essential in the undertaking of their job. It was always impressed upon them that they must protect the security of the drill at all costs. In fact there was a policy that if they mislaid the drill it would cost them £200 to replace it.

This particular engineer was working on a property in a rough part of town. He had used his drill but temporarily put it down and walked around the corner to where his van was parked. On his return the drill had gone. Rather than own up and take his medicine he decided to make it look like his van had been broken into and that the drill had been stolen in the course of the break in. In doing so he was hoping to avoid paying the £200. This idea seemed to resonate with him as this was the last job of the day and the "break in" could happen that evening.

These company vans carried quite a bit of kit and they were very secure. In the course of his poor decision making he elected to enter the back of the van and "break out", rather than to have thought it through and actually "broken in" to the van from the outside. In the course of doing he caused several hundred pounds worth of damage. He then phoned the office to report the "break in" and was told to take the vehicle to the designated repair workshop to get the damage repaired. He also reported that his drill had been taken as a result of the "break in".

The repair workshop was very keen to keep the business of a large company and subsequently reported that there were inconsistencies with the reported damage to this van. They provided a report to say that under no circumstances was this van broken into as reported by the engineer. It had very definitely been damaged by someone from the inside.

The engineer had managed to contrive a situation where he had turned the simple theft of his drill [which would have cost him £200] into a situation whereby he had caused hundreds of pounds of criminal damage to a company vehicle and was now falsifying documents to pretend that the van had been broken into. He had effectively turned a criminal act by someone else into a several criminal offences perpetrated by himself. The evidence against him was however overwhelming and despite a futile attempt to continue to try to lie his way out of it his employment was terminated.

***

Working closely with the security department you did get to hear about some funny stories relating to those burgling the company stores. Whilst not really a specific HR issue, they are amusing and worthy of repeating.

In one of our Swindon units security microphones were fitted in the walls of the building so that the supplier of the alarm system could monitor the audio to hear whether anyone was using force to break in. One burglar broke in through the roof but being somewhat incompetent was unable to get out of the store. He had little alternative but to telephone the Police to ask them to come and arrest him. During the time that he was waiting for their arrival the microphones picked him up rehearsing what he would say to the Police. They included, 'it's a fair cop Guv', 'I'm just a little early for the sales', and 'One minute I was looking for a vacuum, the next minute the lights had been turned off I was locked in!'

In another store one of the local burglars was in the habit of taking his Pitbull out on burglaries for protection. He was a horrible character who had already used the dog to attack civilians on two occasions. Having broken in to the store he set off the silent alarms alerting the police. A police dog handler arrived with a great big German Shepherd and the burglar made the mistake of trying to get his Pitbull to attack both the officer and the police dog. It was literally a fatal error as the Pitbull was killed by the Police dog and the burglar easily arrested.

***

Normally when dealing with people who were subject to disciplinary hearings or investigations I always made the point of treating them decently. I was always polite and reasonable even when I knew they were lying through their teeth. It never helped the cause to be antagonistic towards the subject.

One person who tested this professional 'decency' was responsible for the next story. I preface this by saying that this is another of those stories that if you were not involved you would not possibly believe. I can however confirm that it is 100% true.

The company employed hundreds of engineers whose job was to visit a customer's house to install the product. Typically the installation would take perhaps one hour, give or take half an hour either side.

I'll call the engineer in question Darren Richards and the first that I had heard about Darren was when I received a telephone call from the "representative" of the customer Mrs Smith. I took the "representative" to be a friend of Mrs Smith rather than a solicitor or lawyer. They alleged that an engineer had attended the Mrs Smith's house and behaved in an indecent way, furthermore he said that they had physical evidence of his behaviour. He told me that Mrs Smith was not in good health, was badly asthmatic and needed to constantly to be connected to an oxygen supply in her daily life.

I told the representative that we would thoroughly investigate any such conduct and could he please tell me what the evidence was. He refused to tell me but said that it was in the hands of the police. I explained that we would need to put the evidence to our employee to investigate this matter properly and to get his response before we could take any action. It was imperative that we could show the engineer the evidence. We eventually agreed that I would contact the police and speak to them before proceeding.

The allegation was so serious that we had no alternative but to suspend Darren Richards pending a full investigation. In the meantime I spoke to the police and they confirmed that there was an allegation of indecent exposure and that the whole episode had been recorded by the customer Mrs Smith. On payment of £40 the police agreed to release the transcript of the conversation between Mrs Smith and our engineer.

The transcript duly arrived on my desk and from that plus other further enquiries, a clearer picture of events started to emerge. The engineer had gone to the customer's property and had started the installation. Within a matter of minutes he had started to make comments about her breasts which made her feel very uncomfortable and particularly so in view of her poor health. Whilst he returned to his van to get some tools, thinking quickly she got a tape recorder and placed it on top of a wardrobe. The tape recorder clearly picked up the full conversation for a period of about 40 minutes thereafter.

Darren Richards was heard to say, `Is there any chance that I could have a look at your breasts`?

Mrs Smith replied with a very definite `No you cannot`.

Richards did not give up at this point and during the course of fitting the product kept asking if he could see Mrs Smith's breasts. He told her that he had never seen breasts. This in itself was bizarre as he was a married man!

The total drivel flowing from the engineer's mouth continued. He must have asked the same question at least twenty times, sometimes slightly re-phrased, always re-buffed by Mrs Smith. Sometimes pleading, sometimes claiming that he was disadvantaged and naive, he persisted. This line of one sided conversation must have carried on for twenty pages of typed A4 paper.

At one point he had to telephone the engineering department with his identification number so that the system could be tested. In doing so there was absolutely clear evidence that it was his voice on the tape and he was the person in the property.

This must have been an extremely worrying time for the customer Mrs Smith. The tape did not suggest that Darren Richards was physically threatening, if anything he was more pleading and begging. That said, it must have been very concerning for a female in her own home, in poor health and on oxygen, to be faced with this behaviour.

Richards wasn't finished and turned his line of questioning to his own anatomy. He said, ` Is there any chance that you could have a look at my er.....old man?`

`What do you mean?` said Mrs Smith

He replied `Well can you look at my todger, my....errr.....thingy....?`

Mrs Smith again rebuffed him the strongest possible terms. I suppose that she could have called the police or the company but she did not do so. I can only guess that she was very shocked and stressed by the incident.

Once again this request to look at private parts went on for a further twenty pages of A4 transcript and culminated with him producing his penis and disappearing into another room. It is probably fortunate that the tape recorder was now out of range although the total transcript of this incident ran into about 45 pages of A4. Quite clearly the events were very disturbing indeed as this individual had been with the company for a number of years and through his job was routinely required to visit customers in their homes.

As sometimes happens in these matters the police did not have enough grounds to pursue a prosecution against the `perpetrator`. I spoke to them in some detail about the case and as he was invited into the house and exposed himself in a private residence not in the street, there was not enough evidence to prosecute. I understand that this decision will seem astonishing to most people and it did to me.

Whilst there was no action under the criminal law the issue of whether he contravened company policy was a whole separate issue. It is fairly common for an employee to subject to both a police investigation and a company investigation. From the company point of view the two things are treated separately. The police investigation is totally outside of your control and normally you have limited access to all the evidence gathered.

In HR terms you have to conduct your own investigation and then consider whether there are grounds for the individual to face a disciplinary hearing. You will look at any evidence available and obtain witness statements. Documentary evidence is vital as employment tribunals love documents. Perhaps there are receipts or invoices, contracts of employment, company policies or a contract of employment to consider.

In dealing with employment issues which involve criminality you do not however have to prove the case beyond reasonable doubt as you do in a court of law. You have to conduct a full investigation followed by a disciplinary hearing at which the employee has the opportunity to put their side of the case. There are also certain rights which have to be observed such as them being accompanied by a colleague or trade union representative and a right of appeal against the decision. It is also absolutely essential that you comply with your own policies and procedures.

Darren Richards was required to attend an internal company investigation meeting which he refused to do. Instead he tendered his resignation initially providing one months notice. As he had given one months notice I again required him to attend the investigation. Again he refused to do so and resigned with immediate effect.

Once an employee has resigned with immediate effect there is no longer a contract with the company and absolutely nothing that the company can do with regard to investigation or disciplinary action.

***

I recall being involved in a case where two members of staff had committed a fairly obvious theft when they were videoed stealing an expensive roll of carpet from company premises. An investigation was conducted and they summoned to a disciplinary hearing and subsequently dismissed for gross misconduct for the misappropriation of the carpet. They appealed against the decision but were unsuccessful. They were subsequently arrested by the police and charged with the theft. When they got to court they were found not guilty. They subsequently tried to take the matter to employment tribunal but were unsuccessful because the company had conducted a fair investigation according to its policies and procedures and acted reasonably in making the decision to dismiss.

***

In a large company occasionally you have employees imprisoned for offences which occurred out of work time on matters unrelated to work. Normally you had not heard about these matters in advance as they probably hoped that they would "get off" and that no one would ever find out at work. For example I have known employees imprisoned for drug dealing. If this happens "by surprise" technically you still have an employment contract with them and it is likely that they will be receiving pay and benefits which is all an expense to the company when they are incapable of turning up for work. Normally action needs to be taken to terminate that contract once you have ascertained all the facts of the matter.

***

It is also not unusual for employees during the course of their normal employment to become involved as witnesses in criminal court cases and this can have a very detrimental effect on their personal life outside of work.

I recall one very sad incident when a manager witnessed a theft from his store and tried to heroically stop the offender. Not a big man, during the course of the incident he was assaulted and the offender made off. He subsequently was asked to attend the police station for an identification parade to try to pick out the suspect. Normally in such cases the police have to be scrupulously careful about how the identification parade is conducted, for example they must absolutely avoid the suspect and witness coming into contact at the location where parade is being arranged.

Unfortunately for our manager a serious mistake was made and he and the suspect were let into the police station and ended up in the same waiting room. He was then assaulted by the suspect within the confines of the police station and threats were made about him attending court as a witness. Being a determined character he decided that he would attend court to see justice done and he gave evidence on both the theft and the two assaults. The individual was subsequently sent to prison for two years but that wasn`t the end of the matter. Two days later the manager returned home from work to find that his home had been burgled and many personal possessions trashed including his children`s toys etc. The perpetrators had even taken a spade and attacked the plaster on the walls of the children`s bedrooms. This was a frightening experience and clearly organised by the individual who had just been convicted.

11 DEATH, INJURY AND SADNESS

Inevitably when working for large companies, someone in an HR role will deal with events of great sadness or even death. In my experience a workforce of several thousand employees will see at least a few deaths from natural causes during in a year. Furthermore there can be fall out when a tragedy has occurred outside work but affects the work life of the individual.

When an individual dies whilst in the employment of the company, one role that needs to be undertaken is for someone to make a report to the pension trustees regarding the payment of any death in service payment. Some company pension schemes pay four times the employee's annual salary to either named beneficiaries or to the estate and therefore it is a significant amount of money.

It never ceases to amaze me how the vultures begin to circle when they start to smell the cash. One assistant manager died suddenly whilst employed by my company. He was a single man in his early sixties without children who was a friendly and popular member of staff. He had told colleagues that he was not in a relationship, did not have any living close relatives and wasn't in touch with any other distant family. He was just happy with his circle of friends.

There were no named beneficiaries in the 'death in service' pension documentation and I needed to get hold of the will so that I could inform the company pension trustees. In order to collect the will, I arranged to meet the executor at the former employee's property as he was involved in arranging for the clearance of personal effects prior to the house sale.

When I arrived some of the deceased's distant family members were also there. They had strong cockney accents, far removed from those in the locality. The collective aurora was that of a pack of vultures picking over a carcass. Obviously they were fairly well briefed with regard to these situations and aware that the company pension scheme could contribute a great deal to the estate. They made what was basically a thinly disguised sales pitch to me, describing how close they were to the deceased, how often they saw each other and that he'd "always said he'd look after them if he went first." This was completely at odds with everything that I had heard. As I always did, I played a `dead bat` and expressed my sincere condolences at their loss. I further confirmed that I would put in a report to the trustees at my earliest opportunity. They "kindly" offered me all of their personal details lest I should forget who they were.

Back in the office I studied the will. It was clear that a great deal of thought and effort had gone into the document and it had been carefully divided it up into thirtieths which were to be allocated to those people who were important to him. There was absolutely no mention of the names of those vultures that I had encountered in the deceased's house. It was fairly clear to me that my recommendation to the trustees would be to make the payment of around £60,000 to his estate which would be distributed in accordance with his wishes expressed in his will. I'm sure that the vultures would not have left empty handed, but at least it would have been with an old washing machine rather than his cash.

**

Sometimes people have to cope with terrible tragedy and I recall another sad tale from a colleague. This particular lady was in her early forties, held a managerial position with the company and seemed very happy in her working life. In her personal life she was divorced and probably a little `jaundiced` by experiences.

The one subject that always brought a smile to her face and a twinkle to her eye was the subject of her only son. He was seventeen and had decided to join the army and was waiting for his start date. I recall her telling me that whilst she was pleased that he had found a sense of purpose, she was particularly worried that he may be posted to Northern Ireland. I tried to reassure her by saying that whilst it was a dangerous place thousands of servicemen and women had undertaken tours of duty and returned unscathed.

Not long after this I left the company and moved on to pastures new. A few months later I will never forget turning on the national news to see that her son had been killed in an explosion within weeks of being posted to Northern Ireland.

***

In another terrible event a member of staff was driving in a car and following his son who was riding ahead on a motorbike. Tragically the motorbike was involved in a head on collision and the son was killed. The father was literally yards away when it happened. It is impossible to comprehend how people recover from such loss.

***

During my career employees have come to me for help when they have major issues in their private life and they feel that they have no one who can help. I have never forgotten one such case involving a young woman who was subject to a violent and abusive relationship.

Early one morning there was a knock on my office door and stood there was Nella. She was a very pretty dark skinned Mauritian woman and spoke with a French accent. She had not been employed by the company for long but had already gained a reputation as an excellent worker.

I asked her to come in and could immediately see bruising on her face and a painful looking swelling to her forehead. She had clearly been crying. I asked her to stay where she was whilst I got the trained first aider to attend to her injuries.

After the first aider had attended to her and left the room, I gently asked her to explain what had happened. She told me that she had met her husband in Mauritius whilst he was on holiday and that he had brought her back to England where they had got married. They had only known each other for 12 months or so and he worked at a local hospital as porter.

She said that not long after they were married he had become violent towards her and not only that, but he had offered her to men for money. She wanted to leave her husband and had spoken to her sisters but they had implored her to stay with him as it would have brought great shame on the family. As there was no one that she could turn to someone from work had suggested that she came to see me in HR. The final straw for her was the beating that he had inflicted that morning because she had refused to be prostituted to another man.

To see this young lady covered in bruises and with no one to help was heartbreaking and I told her that I was not prepared to stand by and let this situation continue. At that point I hadn't dealt with anything quite like this before but I had heard of women's refuges and decided to contact one to see if they could help.

When I telephoned the refuge I explained the situation and asked them if I could drive her up to their premises that day. Of course they could not give their location away so I arranged to meet them at a neutral place and took Nella with me. The women working at the refuge were absolutely fantastic. Most importantly they took her in and gave her an immediate place of safety where she could stay until she had the opportunity to find a more permanent home.

She never did return to the abusive husband and within a few weeks started to slowly regain her confidence. It is now more than twenty-five years on since then and I still have the thank you card that she gave me. Often in HR you are the bearer of bad news about redundancy or dismissal etc. In this case it was just good to know that you made a positive difference to someone's life.

***

Terminal illness is another issue which will raise its head in any large organisation. Care and consideration for the employee is of paramount importance and it is not long before the HR department is asked to provide information about any insurance payments that will be available to the next of kin. Quite often these come via a death in service scheme or a separate pension scheme.

The death in service scheme that I was familiar with paid out four times salary in the event of death whilst still employed by the company. This was of some comfort to the employee if they had family left behind. Occasionally the terminally ill employee did not have family and in those cases sometimes the insurance company could be persuaded to make a payment before death so that they could gain some benefit before they died. Often this was only 25% of the figure that they would have received after death but at least it could be put to good use.

We were able to arrange this for one young man in his early thirties who was diagnosed with terminal cancer. He was someone who lived alone but did not want to spend his last months waiting for the inevitable. He asked if he could work until the last opportunity and the company was able to arrange this for him. It did strike me as being somewhat sad that he had nothing better to do than to spend his last weeks and months at work but if it gave him some comfort or took his mind off things then so be it.

12 TRAINING COURSES, WHY?

I will preface this very short chapter by saying that for the next couple of pages my tongue is very firmly in my cheek.

If I am being honest, I have attended and presented literally hundreds of training courses. Obviously most training is extremely useful and should be embraced. I do however have a few gripes with the way that training courses used to be administered. Why did they always cram so much into the day that there was barely enough time to get a shower? How often did you complete a packed day, pause for dinner, and then have to prepare a presentation until midnight?

Many companies use good quality hotels for these things with gyms etc. What's the point when there is never time to use them? When there is a lot to cram in why is so much wasted on silly `ice-breakers` like making people stand in a line in order of height...or age....or shoe size......! At the end of a course where people have travelled hundreds of miles to get there, why do we have to leave so late on a Friday afternoon?

Why does the HR department sometimes flirt with too much `pop psychology?` I remember one management course having to step on a serious of squares on the floor and on each square I had to imagine and state that I was a different object. I had to take a step on a square and say something like, `I am a balloon`, then another step and say `I am a picture..`. What on earth did that do for me in order to better prepare me for management? When I was sitting in the classroom at 4.30pm on a Friday with 200 miles to travel I would be thinking why did we waste an hour on that, we could be gone by now!

Why do they always want me to build a raft and then get drenched when it doesn`t float? When do we always have to gather around another bloody flip chart? Why do they do the `creeping death` introductions at the start of a course when people are all a bit tense? Why, when retail managers give their ages during those introductions, do they always look older than they are?

Another particularly annoying and disturbing part of certain HR management courses was their seeming attempt to get people to bear their souls in front of the group. This may be in the course of telling the group about weaknesses or stressful life events etc. I saw numerous people, especially females, reduced to tears in this way. Personally I don`t go to work to bear my soul, I`ll do that in my time, thank you!

The test for me when evaluating the success or otherwise of a training course was threefold, `did I learn anything, will this change my behaviour or approach and will it contribute to the profitability of the company`. If all three questions were met with a `yes` then it was not time wasted.

13 SICKNESS, ABSENCE AND WASTERS

Most large companies will always have a number of employees who are sick, the vast majority will be genuine people. There are also a percentage who fall into the category whereby they are so ill that there is little chance of them ever returning to the workplace. Typically they run out of company sick pay and at some point their employment is terminated unless there is an option for a medical pension or an insurance related payment.

One of the most annoying categories are the people who are incapable of attending work on a regular basis because they are, well, fundamentally lazy! Ooooh I've said it, how naughty of me! These are the people who will be disciplined for their poor attendance and if it doesn't improve end up with the company medical department [in the case of larger companies] or get dismissed.

Now in fairness, some of these people do have bad backs etc which are ok one day and painful the next. Some people are just 'wasters' swinging the lead and have done so at every company that they've worked for. The one thing that is certain is that the additional work and pressure is always picked up by people who are very rarely absent.

One bizarre example of a 'waster' was an individual who worked in sales at a previous company. He was forever on sick leave, never for any one particular reason but for a multitude of reasons including the usual flu, migraine, bad back, sickness, diarrhoea etc etc. The most that he ever worked was about 3 days per week and if every company was staffed with people like him they would go under.

To cut a long story short, I was obliged to go through the exhaustive sickness absence policy with him which at the time, involved a number of disciplinary hearings and visits to the company doctor.

Eventually after several months his attendance did not improve and he was eventually dismissed for his poor attendance/ill health. This was a relief for both his manager and myself as he had been a pain in the backside.

Anyway the business that I was working in was fairly `incestuous` with workers moving between the various competitors with some regularity to enhance their careers etc. Every now and then the industry would be prone to takeovers whereby a larger company snapped up a smaller company. From an HR point of view this would lead to redundancies depending upon where the branches were located in a particular town.

When these sorts of things happened I was one of the first to see a list of staff and salaries of the newly acquired company. From a quick scan down the list I could see that I had re-acquired the individual who I had dismissed a matter of months before from my own organisation. I immediately checked his attendance with our newly acquired company and could see that he had already taken excessive sick leave for pretty much the same variety of reasons as those for which I had already recently sacked him.

Whilst it was a shock for me to see the name of a recently dismissed person on the staff listing of the new company, I`m sure that it was more of a shock for him to see my name as his new HR Manager. It was only a matter of weeks before I had to sack him for the second time that year. He remains the only person that I have ever dismissed twice in the same year from different companies.

***

Now normally the issue of taking excessive sickness leave as an alternative to holiday, as was specific to the odd individual. In colloquial terms it is of course known as `throwing a sickie` or something similar. I did however uncover a department whereby things were a little more organised.

I had joined a new company and was spending the first weeks going around the various company units throughout the region that I was covering. One such unit was an engineering department in Wales. I arrived one morning and was generally meeting the staff and having a walk around.   I had a list of the names of supervisors and was keen to try to speak to all of them so that I could put a name to a face and get a better understanding of the business.

I normally paid such visits in the company of the local area manager but would always seek to spend some time talking to the staff out of their earshot to get an unbiased view of HR issues in the department. I used to have the habit of trying to remember names of anyone that I came into contact with and at least one piece of information about them.   It didn`t have to be anything work orientated, it could be a hobby or interest or the name of their partner.   I was speaking to one of the engineers and having a general chat about work and hobbies etc and I decided to ask him about his supervisor whose name I had remembered.

I said, `Bill Smith, is your supervisor isn`t he, is he around today`?

`No, he`s on the sick rota today`.

I was a little taken aback by this comment.   Did he actually say `sick rota?`   Giving him the benefit of the doubt I said `Oh, sorry to hear that, what`s wrong with him?`

He replied `Nothing, we just rota the sickness here it`s a bit fairer.`

I could not believe what I`d just heard.   An employee had just confirmed to his HR Manager that there was a formal `sick rota` in place so that people could actually fairly rota their sick leave!   It transpired that the reason that they organised themselves was to both ensure that the appropriate amount of `sick leave` was taken so that they didn`t lose out on company sick pay, and that it was apportioned fairly.   Needless to say the sick rota became consigned to history!

***

One issue that raised its head fairly often regarding absence involved employees from India and Pakistan.   For them it was very expensive to go home for one or two weeks so they would sometimes ask for extended six week holiday periods.   Certainly in the 1980`a and 1990`s many companies did not allow such absence and did not want to set a precedent by allowing it.

It often led to a bizarre game of `cat and mouse` whereby they would put in a request for an extended holiday of six weeks which would be refused in accordance with the prevailing company policy which allowed for a maximum of two weeks. They would then need to take two weeks as holiday and then "go sick" for the rest of the time. Those who were clever would "fall ill" in India or Pakistan and fax back a medical note.

Those who were not so clever would take two weeks holiday and remain abroad for a further 4 weeks. They would then get a friend to phone in sick on their behalf from the UK and say that they would provide the doctor`s certificate in due course after they had been to the doctor. When the doctor`s certificate did not turn up after a further 8 days the company would try to contact them to see if they were OK. Sometimes one of the managers would pop round to the house to see how they were but they were never in, they were always out "at the doctors".

I recall one bizarre case involving JT Fidla. He had been turned down for extended holiday but then took the 2 week holiday followed by 4 week sickness. Of course what complicates these matters is if the person is confirmed to be lying and stating that they are sick when they are not, they can be getting paid company sick pay. In other words they are fraudulently claiming company sick pay by deception.

JT was certainly not at home for a month whilst he was claiming to be sick and was clearly abroad. On his eventual return he produced a sick certificate from a "Dr Livingstone" to cover his complete four week absence after the period when his holiday finished. A quick check with the surgery confirmed that the doctor did not exist and clearly the certificate had been either stolen or forged which proved terminal for JT`s employment.

***

Indeed in my career I saw quite of number of altered medical certificates and falsified company sickness documentation. Normally it was a very poor job whereby the dates had just been changed.

Others made false claims such as that they had `twisted their ankle` and gone to hospital A and E. If they did so using formal company documentation and it was found to be false, they had falsified a document to claim company sick pay.   Always the result was dismissal.   Both hospitals and doctors do tend to record events so these claims are normally disprovable if they are false.

***

Occasionally a sickness absence case could be complicated by the fact that the person was absent from their main work at our company, but seemingly very capable of being able to undertake part-time work for another employer.

One such employee had a bad back and apparently could not work as an engineer. He could however work as a DJ on the weekend and carry around heavy cases of records.

Someone else couldn't work during the week but could front a T-Rex tribute band on weekends. Funny that, their colleagues are placed under the strain of doing extra work yet they miraculously become fit for the weekend but then incapacitated for Monday-Friday!   Over the years I have noticed that those carrying the load become increasingly frustrated with those `swinging the lead`.

***

One of the most breathtaking `lead-swinging` cases that I came across involved an employee based in the Midlands. He was employed as an installer but had been signed off from work for six weeks with a bad back. Well I have an occasional bad back and it is extremely painful. There would be no chance whatsoever that I could play football with it. Our man however, was well enough to be able to play, even when signed off work!

Not only was he capable of playing football he was also capable of having an altercation on the pitch and getting sent off. When the match finished he waited for his rival in the changing rooms and assaulted him causing Grievous Bodily Harm. He was subsequently arrested and charged and taken to court. Not much of a back problem me thinks....!

14 THE EXIT DOOR

When people leave a company it can be a stressful experience, even if it is just straight forward resignation by that person. When however their employment is terminated and it is not their choice to do so, that stress is magnified many fold.

Redundancy is a case in point. In practice the definition of redundancy is when a job ceases, diminishes or moves to another location. An example of a job ceasing would be where a manufacturing company with several factories around the country moves production in one factory to another factory in a different part of the country. Generally speaking a company will make efforts to relocate those employees who wish to make the move, assuming that there are enough jobs at the new location. Also they will not hire new staff at the new place until a process of consultation has been completed with existing employees in the redundant factory.

The consultation process normally involved seeking volunteers for redundancy. For certain employees that was often an appealing scenario particularly if it allowed them to retire early or to perhaps gain a lump sum to use to retrain or travel etc. Consultation may involve redeploying people to other positions within the business normally with a trial period to see if the change was acceptable to both sides. In some cases consultation was a `box-ticking` exercise where everyone knew that there was no hope of anything but redundancy at the end of it.

Such was the case in another redundancy scenario where business at a retail store in one location was hit by competition and recession and it was now uneconomic to continue. The Area Manager was new to his position and had not dealt with redundancy before. The store was in a part of Wales where it was very difficult to find work. When the senior management had taken a decision to close the store we were despatched to deliver the bad news. For a location such as this, there was no chance of redeploying the staff within a reasonable travelling distance. Our job was to make the announcement and then begin a process of consultation with little realistic chance of a positive outcome for the employees.

On the journey to the store I tried to reassure him that in my experience if you treated people with dignity and respect and went the extra mile in trying to do everything in your power to help them as much as possible, they normally responded reasonably well after the initial shock of the news.

On arrival we gathered the employees together and made the announcement. Obviously there was a degree of shock in spite of what they must have been witnessing in terms of takings and customer flow. We then arranged to see the staff individually to start the consultation. The first member of staff we saw was a 16 hour a week part time female employee. If any group of people reacted in a reasonable way it was normally this profile of person, she didn't. She went ballistic, bouncing off the walls and screaming blue murder for about ten minutes! The newly appointed area manager was ashen during this performance and probably not looking forward to the rest of his career! Eventually she calmed down and the rest of the staff proved to be very accepting of the news as they had seen the way that the business had been diminishing over previous weeks.

***

One of the saddest forms of dismissal is where someone is dismissed because they are no longer able to do the job for which they were employed. This is not usually a short process, it often takes many months or even stretches into years. Normally this only occurs after every avenue is explored with company doctors. The sorts of things that are considered are a gradual return to the work place, reducing their hours, changing their job, looking at any aids that may help such as changes to the workspace etc.

At some point those on long term sick are likely to run out of company sick pay and have exhausted the possibilities listed above. You then have the scenario when they remain on the company books but are not being paid. Indeed they may still be in receipt of company benefits. At this point it is usual for the company to terminate their employment.

I recall one case which I inherited when I joined a company. This person had exhausted all opportunities for rehabilitation or a return to the work place and had run out of sick pay. She had been absent for around two years and was not even known to the manager of the store who had been in position for 18 months.

Her reason for being off sick was due to injuries received in falling off a cliff. She was apparently out walking with her husband and the next thing she knew she was being airlifted to hospital. She had no recollection of the moments before she fell. It wasn't clear whether she slipped and fell, was depressed or was even pushed. Whatever the scenario, I had to terminate her employment and she exited the company.

***

Not everyone that you deal with is a pleasure. Some people are desperate to leave the company but cannot face the fact that they could simply resign. They are determined to try and get a payment for doing so. One such person worked in the Midlands region and was of Turkish extraction. He had a simply terrible sick record but the policies of the company at that time were fairly soft and contained various trigger points whereby action would only be taken after a trigger point was reached.

Those that knew the trigger points would play the system, one of whom was my Turkish friend. He would take the maximum sickness possible all the time avoiding the trigger points and all the time trying to get a payoff for his "poor health." His constant sickness had annoyed his colleagues who had to undertake his share of the work when he was off. It is interesting to watch how the initial "good on him" for getting away view of some colleagues, morphs into contempt as everyone has to work significantly harder and there is no extra budget for temporary staff or overtime.

According to his colleagues the main causes of his sickness were due to the fact that he and his brother had opened a cafe and that he was working in it and claiming to be sick. Unfortunately of course, this was hearsay and it was not possible to prove as no one would make a statement to that effect.

After a period of time he did go off sick permanently and having exhausted all options of gradual return to work [not that he wanted to return], change of job etc he ran out of sick pay and his employment was terminated. Whilst he received only his notice pay he had been a constant thorn in the side of management causing a disproportionate amount of time to be spent of his case. He also caused stress and extra work to his colleagues.

That said he did have a degree of charm and having sorted out his notice payment he kindly invited me round for a Turkish coffee. Now that was fairly unlikely as the 100 mile journey slightly put me off as did the thought of spending any more time talking to him!

It was some months later I heard that the business was in trouble and soon after I received a telephone call from him.

`Hello it`s Engin, hey you never did pop round for a coffee.`

`Err no,` I replied, `I`ve been a bit busy this last few months.`

`I was just wondering, is there any chance of my old job back?` he said.

`I thought that a few months ago you were really ill and totally incapable of working?` I said.

`Everything is better now,` he replied `I`ll take any medical examination. What do you think are the chances of me coming back, I spoke to my old manager and he said ring you.`

I said, `you want me to tell you the chances of you returning to work for us?`

`Yes, what are the chances of a return,` he said.

`In the circumstances, none at all` I replied with a smile.

`Why don`t you come up for a Turkish coffee and we can discuss it?`

`I`m a bit busy,` I replied.

He laughed and understood exactly where I was coming from.

15 THE DREADED TRIBUNAL

By way of background to this section, an Employment Tribunal [formerly known as an Industrial Tribunal] is a judicial body which was established to hear claims about matters pertaining to employment. There are a huge number of employment related issues which can be settled at tribunal and these include such matters as claims for unfair dismissal, redundancy payments, discrimination, non-payment of wages etc. You could find Tribunals regionally situated throughout England, Wales and Scotland, normally in the major cities of a region, such as London, Birmingham, Exeter, Cardiff, Southampton etc. In the UK employment disputes which do not get settled between the employer and employee will ultimately end up in Employment Tribunal.

When you attend tribunal to give evidence you will normally find that there is a panel of 3 people. The tribunal Chair is legally qualified and the most important and influential person on the panel and tends to direct proceedings. In addition to the Chair you will normally find two lay members of the tribunal. The lay members are appointed by Government Ministers and have experience in dealing with work related problems. One lay member will normally have experience in representing employees, for example this can be someone with trade union experience. The other lay member will be someone with a managerial background, for example someone who has experience of employing staff.

An Employment Tribunal is like a court but is not quite as formal, for example the tribunal Chair does not wear a wig or a gown. In addition an individual can bring the case themselves and act as their own advocate if they so wish. Many people are anxious about giving evidence at tribunal because the story may end up in a newspaper. In my experience the vast majority of cases are of little interest to the press unless someone has told them that there will be a good story available!

If you are involved in a case involving discrimination that can still be fairly newsworthy and you may find that the papers get hold of the detail. Is it very disconcerting for a manager to find their working life scrutinized in the local or even national newspaper.

With over twenty years experience of dealing with employment issues for some of the largest companies in the country, some of these issues inevitably ended up at tribunal. Of those that did go to tribunal, I was lucky enough to act as the advocate for the company in many cases. In numerous other cases I was a witness or sometimes just the company representative whilst the matter was handled by lawyers.

Of course the first time that you act as advocate for a company is quite stressful. It is effectively like being a QC but without the training. Whilst I was familiar with both a court setting and employment law, the first time that I presented a tribunal was quite eventful. The case involved a claim of race discrimination against the company from a Libyan man named `Omar` who was employed on a part-time basis in a retail store. Essentially he was complaining that the manager was overlooking him for promotion and that he was being `put upon` by the manager by being asked to undertake tasks which other staff members did not have to do.

I was familiar with this individual as we had made a great deal of effort to develop his skills and to put him on available training courses in the previous 12 months. In fact he had received more time and effort to development him than anyone else in the store. His performance in that time did not suggest that he was ready for career progression and in any case there were no opportunities in his locality.

It was one of those unfortunate situations in a working life where at that particular time, all avenues were closed. Whilst it is frustrating it does not mean that they will be closed forever. On many occasions I have seen what appears to be a bit of a "log jam" change. It only takes one person to get promotion or to leave, or for the company to decide to build another store, or for a special project to become available. Someone such as Omar would have been well advised to have stayed put and worked as hard as possible to make himself the number candidate for any future opportunities. Either that or he had the choice to leave. Instead of these options he saw the £££ signs and decided to launch a fairly frivolous and vexatious employment tribunal claim.

Part of his claim was that the store manager had threatened to throw him out of a second floor window and had made him carry heavy shelving up some stairs. Whilst the manager was in his mid-fifties, not in particularly good health and weighing about nine stones, Omar was a fit and healthy man in his mid-twenties. He was probably six feet tall and weighed at least 12 ½ stones.

I found it very hard to believe that he seriously threatened Omar and when I asked him about this he told me that Omar had referred to English women as "tarts, whores and easy lays" and that as he had a daughter of seventeen, he said it as a rebuff to this comment but not in any way meaning it or indeed, being capable of doing it. The manager also told me that the shelving that he was asked to lift was light and that all staff members were used to moving it around the store as goods were continually being re-merchandised.

I was left with the impression that this was some who was `chancing his arm` in bringing a race discrimination claim because he had been motivated by the unlimited damages which success in the matter would bring. In fact he brought the claim whilst remaining employed and in the knowledge that at that time tribunals rarely awarded costs against a claimant and that effectively it was a `free pot-shot` against the company.

As previously mentioned, this was the first time that I was to act as advocate at a tribunal. This responsibility brought some pressure as all race discrimination cases were reported to the Board of Directors of what was a very large company. It would not have been good for my career had I failed. Not only that but as the vast majority of tribunals are open to the public and the press, this case came with the possibility that anyone appearing may become the subject of unwanted media attention.

I made the decision that in presenting this case I would be as prepared as I possibly could be. In the weeks before the case I spent hours and hours studying the documentation and made sure that I knew it inside out. I also spent time with the manager to try to coach him before his appearance in the witness box. He found the whole event so stressful that he ended up on prescription medication. This is the unseen sort of collateral damage that is never, ever, considered by a tribunal. In my view a decent man who is the subject of a false claim suffering damage to his health.

As part of my preparation on the morning of the tribunal I visited the store and collected 2-3 shelves which Omar claimed were allegedly heavy and difficult to carry. I put these in the boot of my car and headed to the tribunal office building. The Employment Tribunal building was in a large ten storey block and when I arrived I took the lift to the top floor. As it was a regional office there were perhaps 8-10 tribunal rooms in which they could hear numerous cases all at the same time.

I walked down the corridor looking for the names of the company on the door to identify my room. As I walked along I passed one room where the public gallery was packed and indeed there were spectators 3 deep standing at the back. I wondered for a moment what sort of case could attract such a large crowd. I carried on past several more tribunal rooms to the end of the corridor but could not find our case name written on the door. It suddenly dawned on me that this was my case. My first case as an advocate had attracted a large crowd indeed! After taking a few deep breaths and accompanied by a pile of documents and a couple of shelves I entered the room.

I took my place and shortly after the tribunal Chairman and his two colleagues entered the room. The clerk asked the assembled people to stand and they duly did before the Chairman took his seat. After each side briefly outlined their case Omar took the witness stand to provide his evidence. He seemed to revel in the fact that he was centre of attention and the audience was mainly female. Whilst I may be regarded as biased, he came across as arrogant and a little smarmy.

After 2-3 hours I had the opportunity to cross examine him on his evidence. I asked him to describe the shelving which he had been asked to carry up the stairs. He replied `it was very heavy and sharp grey shelving which I could not carry.`

I said, `Can you turn to your right and confirm whether that it a piece of the shelving?`

`Yes,` he replied

`Can you see if you can pick it up for the tribunal?` I said.

`I`ll try,` he said, and easily picked it up.

`That didn`t seem too difficult,` I said.

`It was OK,` he replied.

`Can you pick it up using one hand as well?`

He demonstrated that he could pick it up using one hand.

I continued, `so are you seriously asking this tribunal to believe that this is too heavy for you to carry?`

`Well it is quite heavy,` he said.

`But you could manage it one handed couldn`t you?` I said.

`Well yes`. he said.

I then asked him, `Do you often refer to English women as…[pause]…tarts whores and easy lays?` I fully expected him to deny this as it was the reason that his manager caused him to say that he wanted to throw him out of the window.

Instead he replied, `Well sometimes….I refer to them as tarts.`

There was an audible gasp of disapproval from the assembled women in the public gallery and I left a suitably long gap to let this be digested before I started my next question. The long and the short of it is that he did not come over as a credible witness because he did not have a credible case. After some very uncomfortable hours in the witness box for Omar the case was adjourned for the day.

We had been worried about possible press coverage for both personal reasons and company reasons but were pleased to see that the only negative comment in the national press was directed at Omar, next to a sizeable photo of him with the heading, "Libyan calls English women tarts whores and easy lays!". We turned up for the following day to discover that he had withdrawn his case and that the second planned day was cancelled.

In this sort of case there no winners. It was a weak case brought by someone who was having a pot shot at the company in the hope of getting some cash. In the course of doing so he had caused a lot of work and stress and detrimentally affected the health of his manager.

***

Another memorable tribunal that I was involved in involved a very strange case. I used to work very closely with the security manager and one day he came into my office with a pile of telephone records relating to one of my branches.

He said `We have a problem with someone phoning live sex lines from one of your Devon branches. There are 700 calls in the space of 18 months at a cost to the company of £750.`

I looked at the pile of papers and could see that there were numerous `0898` numbers highlighted in marker pen. This was the old premium rate code which prefaced a number which cost an arm and a leg to phone.

I said `How do you know that these are for live sex lines?`

He replied `Well that`s what they are, all these 0898 numbers are for that sort of stuff although we`ll have to ring a couple as part of the investigation`.

I said `OK, let`s do a couple now while we`re both here so no one can accuse us of doing the same thing!`

`That`s a good idea` he replied.

We then had the fairly comical sight of Jim the Security Manager and the HR Manager gathered around a speakerphone dialing 0898 numbers. I phoned the first number and the response was `Hello big boy, this is Nina the naughty nurse`.

`Oh sorry wrong number,` I said as Jim and I fell about laughing.

`Better do one more,` I said and I dialed a second number.

`Hello this is whiplash Wendy how are yoooooou today.`

I quickly put the phone down as Jim and I struggled to keep a professionally straight face. I was only glad that the office cleaner hadn`t come in for the bin whilst we were on the speaker phone!

Jim confirmed that he had been through the rota and that there was a particular person on duty for all of days when the calls were made except for one day when calls appeared to have been made when the store was closed, all the way through the night.

He said `We have a bit of a problem here because the suspect does not have keys to the store and so it couldn`t have been him as he would not have been able to operate the alarm system. Perhaps we have two people at it?`

We kicked the subject around for a while and then decided to check the alarm records for the store to see if there were any unusual happenings on that night. Sure enough there had been a burglary in early evening and a security guard from an independent security company had been employed to remain in the store to safeguard the premises.

We contacted the security company and they immediately launched an investigation. The results of this were that their guard admitted to phoning the sex line because he was bored during the evening. By a strange coincidence he had phoned the same number as the staff member who was the suspect!

Our security manager then went to the store and interviewed the staff member who subsequently confessed to the telephone calls. His only somewhat bizarre defence was that his fingers had developed an addiction to pressing the telephone keys required to phone these 0898 numbers! He added that he had contacted the local addiction help group but they had not seemed very interested. I wonder why?

He duly faced a disciplinary hearing and was subsequently dismissed for gross misconduct. Quite honestly I thought that we had heard the last of him, after all, who could contest a dismissal having admitted to making 700 calls over an 18 month period in work time when they should have been gainfully employed by the company?

It was with some surprise when I received an Employment Tribunal notification stating that he was making a claim against the company for unfair dismissal. Now some people used to do this because they thought that the company may pay them a few hundred pounds rather than employ lawyers to fight the case. He obviously was not aware that we prepared and fought the cases ourselves.

We also had an unwritten rule about what we saw as a `point of principle.` That meant that in certain cases the company would in no circumstances settle the claim before the hearing because in doing so it may impact the overall workforce in some way. For example it could become common knowledge that someone caught doing this sort of thing would get rewarded with a pay off.

It was fairly clear from the outset that we would not make a small settlement payment in this case and that unless he withdrew the claim it would go all the way to a full tribunal hearing. Whether he was aware that if he did go the tribunal the matter could get reported in the local/ national press I do not know however would anyone really want the fact that they had made 700 calls to live sex lines in work time, be publicized to partners, parents, friends and the whole town???

In those days we could opt for what was known as a pre-assessment hearing whereby a tribunal chairman heard the basis of the case and then decided if it was a strong case or not. If they didn`t feel that the case was strong they would issue a `costs warning` against the claimant which meant that if they persevered with the case and lost, they would have the costs awarded against them. It was designed to weed out he weak cases before they were heard in a full tribunal.

As usual I was well prepared for the pre-assessment hearing complete with a list of the calls that the former employee had made. He had a representative to act as advocate for him. His advocate outlined his case as to why he had been unfairly dismissed for making these calls and running up such a large cost to the company. A large part of his defence was that over the course of 18 months he had "only made an average of 2 calls a day," and that wasn`t too excessive in the scheme of things and that dismissal was too harsh a punishment. The second strand to his defence was based on his claim that he effectively had a disorder similar to a gambling habit whereby his fingers automatically dialed the premium number for these live sex lines.

In my view it was one of the most bizarre defences that I had ever heard. Would the tribunal chair, who happened to be female, accept that this was a reasonable thing to do? After his advocate had finished I rose to my feet and outlined the number, regularity and cost of the calls. Before I finished I quickly added, `Let me just list some of the numbers that were called. Nina the naughty nurse, Whiplash Wendy, Raucous Ruby......,`

`I think I`ve heard enough` said the tribunal chairwoman! It was a very short adjournment indeed before the claimant was issued with a costs warning due to the weakness of his case. The decision had the effect which we were looking for which was for him to withdraw his claim.

At tribunal prior to the case you were always shown to a room in which you could prepare immediately before the hearing and you would never see `the other side` until you entered the room where the hearing was to take place. This was always a good idea as in the preceding months there were often some acrimonious exchanges before the matter went to tribunal. After the case however you could leave the tribunal office and often bump into your adversary on the way out of the building in the lift. In the above case there was a ten floor lift journey down to the ground floor. As we bumped into the claimant in the lift there was a fairly stony silence and much looking at the floor.....mainly by him!

***

I still don`t know why some people feel aggrieved when they have been dismissed, well at least enough to want to go to employment tribunal. If the below case applied to you, would you feel aggrieved enough to make a claim?

You go to a customer`s house as an engineer to make a repair. As you go up to the door you get greeted by a small terrier dog who is barking and being a bit of a nuisance. It is not a Staffordshire or Bull terrier, and not a Pitbull, it is the sort of small dog that poses no threat to you whatsoever and is favoured by the older generation.

In response to this annoying dog you totally lose your marbles and leap over the fence into next doors garden. Once there you try to rip a fence post out of the ground with which to attack the dog. Having acquired a plank of wood, you exit next door`s back gate and then re-enter the gate to the house owned by the customer at which she and her dog lives. Rather than open the gate you kick every wooden panel out of the gate completely shattering it and rendering it useless.

You then start to attack the dog with the plank of wood although luckily the dog is quite quick and starts to run around the small ornate front garden. In the course of swinging the plank at the dog you completely trash the garden causing hundreds of pounds worth of damage. An independent eye witness describes your behavior as like a warrior swinging a samurai sword around his head.

Not surprisingly the customer, a lady in her mid-fifties hears the commotion and runs into the garden to try to get between the dog and you. In the course of this you are still trying to attack the dog. During the melee you swing the wooden gate post towards the dog but hit the lady on the leg causing bruising from her thigh to her calf. Your company liveried van is sitting outside the house advertising the company that you work for.

Well, given those circumstances would you really have been surprised at getting dismissed? With regard to criminal offences you have assaulted a middle aged lady, caused hundreds of pounds of criminal damage damage to a gate and the garden and caused a breach of the peace. From an employment point of view bringing the company into disrepute is one of a very long list of charges.

Anyway, the said individual did get dismissed and did bring a claim to tribunal. The company then incurred great expense in defending and winning the claim and a comical moment of the company lawyer using a tape measure to show the tribunal the height of this tiny animal by the name of `Snuggles.`

***

Having to appear at employment tribunal is very time consuming and costly for the management of a business. A senior manager may well find themselves chairing disciplinary hearings or disciplinary appeals on a very frequent basis. This will only serve to increase their chances of appearing at tribunal. From time to time a security or audit officer or indeed any manager who is charged with conducting a workplace investigation, will find themselves called to give evidence because of their role in an investigation.

If you are an employer, when attending tribunal it is inevitable that you will be facing someone who feels aggrieved by your actions. Sometimes the individual has left the organisation and has struggled to re-establish themselves in employment thereafter, causing much hardship to their family.

It always strikes me as very sad that the once joyful offer and acceptance of employment changes so much when the employment relationship breaks down. Formerly good and cordial relationships can be damaged forever after a visit to tribunal, and the friendship that friends and work colleagues once shared is now gone forever, never to return.

**

16 IN CLOSING

It is fair to say that having joined a company many people are happy to view the HR department from a safe distance. Too many visits to HR will probably not be a good thing, unless of course you work there! It's a bit like the relationship with the village copper, nice to have him the village, not necessarily living next door. This is hardly surprising as the HR Department sometimes has the ability of projecting an image of being a bit of a secretive place in which the darker arts are practiced.

On the one hand HR welcomes you into the company with tea and biscuits, the nice cosy offer of a job and lots of information about pay and benefits. On the other hand we provide you with evidence of your poor performance, boot you out of the company, and then line up to face you in court, a bit like a failed marriage!

From working on the inside in HR, you are provided with a unique insight into human behaviour. The world of employment and making a living is one of the few things in life that we all have in common. The way that people behave in that aspect of their lives will never cease to amaze me.

By its nature the world of Human Resources is crammed full of secrets which some curious members of staff would pay a great deal of money to know. What are the salaries of senior executives? Why was he/she promoted to Operations Director? What actually happened leading up to the dismissal? How was my boss rated at their appraisal? Hopefully this book has given an insight into some of the weird and wonderful events within HR.

My time in Human Resources has been punctuated with hope, expectation, tension, excitement, sadness, disappointment, kindness and frustration in equal measure. There is however, one thing that a career in HR has always delivered, the human stories. Some happy, some sad, some funny and some bad. Just when I think that I have seen it all there is always someone, somewhere, who will do something to surprise me. Long may that continue for anyone contemplating a future in HR.

Was it human resources or was it human remains? I like to think that it was both, and everything in between.

ABOUT THE AUTHOR

After graduating with a degree in Psychology Andrew Wyndham obtained his professional HR qualifications having studied with the Open University. His career included working in the manufacturing, service and retail sectors in the UK.

Printed in Great Britain
by Amazon.co.uk, Ltd.,
Marston Gate.